AMERICAN CREWELWORK

AMERICAN CREWELWORK

Mary Taylor Landon

AND

Susan Burrows Swan

ILLUSTRATED BY

Susan Burrows Swan

THE MACMILLAN COMPANY

COLLIER-MACMILLAN LTD., London

The Macmillan Company
866 Third Avenue, New York, N.Y. 10022
Collier-Macmillan Canada Ltd., Toronto, Ontario

Library of Congress Catalog Card Number: 79-104869

First Printing

Printed in the United States of America

ACKNOWLEDGMENTS

The fabulous collection of needlework at The Henry Francis du Pont Winterthur Museum provided the original inspiration for this book. To adequately thank the many people of that museum who have been so helpful and generous with their time and knowledge is an impossible task. Members of the staff, as well as the museum guides, offered help, guidance, and encouragement.

We particularly want to thank Mrs. Charles Montgomery, Assistant Curator (Textile), who generously shared her vast knowledge with great patience and thoughtfulness in the preparation of the historical section. Charles Hummel, Curator, showed sincere interest in the project and added not only a man's viewpoint, but a most knowledgeable one. Mrs. Richard Terdiman, Editorial Assistant, provided helpful criticism and encouragement and Mrs. Arthur McKelvie, museum guide, made thoughtful suggestions.

Others at the Winterthur Museum who generously aided in the research were Miss Helen Belknap, Librarian of Printed Books, and Mrs. Charles W. Hutton, Assistant Librarian; Mrs. J. Gordon Holt, Librarian of Manuscripts and Microfilm Collection, and her assistant, Mrs. James V. R. Taylor, and Mrs. Dimitrios Fikioris, textile conservator, and her aide, Mrs. John Guthrie.

Mr. Frank L. Horton, Director of Research of The Museum of Southern Decorative Arts, shared his knowledge, as did Miss Mildred Lanier, Assistant Curator of Textiles, Colonial Williamsburg.

Mr. and Mrs. Donald F. Carpenter graciously permitted the illustrator to sketch elements from their superb eighteenth-century American crewel embroidery.

Most of all, our gratitude goes to members of our families. Mary Taylor Landon was encouraged and helped by her husband, George, and their children, Robert B. and Anne Landon Allen. The patience, support and aid given Susan Burrows Swan by her husband, Delmar, and their sons, Douglas and David, will always be appreciated.

SUSAN BURROWS SWAN
MARY TAYLOR LANDON

CONTENTS

I I

HOW TO WORK
CREWEL EMBROIDERY   91

I V

ELEMENTS FOR MAKING YOUR OWN DESIGNS

FOREWORD

During the eighteenth century, American men concerned themselves with the arts of decoration and home furnishing. They commissioned furniture from American cabinetmakers and specified the curtain fabrics and furniture coverings for the rooms of their homes. In 1756, for example, Benjamin Franklin sent printed textiles from London to his wife, Deborah, for a room in their Philadelphia house. Thomas Jefferson, an amateur architect, not only supervised every detail of Monticello, but designed ingenious pieces of furniture and supplied sketches for window curtains. It was a man's world.

In the nineteenth century, women assumed a greater role in matters of home decoration. By the 1850's, books were being published which offered "hints for decorative work." Two such books were: *The Ladies' Hand Book of Fancy and Ornamental Work* (Philadelphia 1859) and *The Ladies' Self Instructor in Millinery and Mantua Making, Embroidery and Appliqué, Canvas-work, Knitting, Netting and Crochet-work* (Philadelphia 1853). Several women's magazines regularly offered patterns for novelties and "tasteful work" of all kinds. Most numerous were the monotonous Berlin wool-work designs to be stitched on canvas.

In 1872 the Royal School of Art Needlework was founded in London to provide "a lucrative and interesting career for women." Inspired by antique embroideries from all countries, new designs were fashioned, often by leading artists, and worked by a corps of skilled embroideresses.

Among the "exhaustless treasures" of the Philadelphia Centennial Exhibition were specially designed and embroidered sets of hangings and panels from the Royal School. The success of this display led to the founding of a needlework school in Philadelphia which contributed to a "resuscitation of one of the valuable arts of the world." As one writer expressed it, "a woman's art, hers by right of inheritance as well as peculiar fitness."

Two leaders, active both in furthering women's education in matters of taste and in bringing about this "efflorescence" of creative needlework, were Mrs. Potter Palmer, President of the Board of Lady Managers at the World's

Columbian Exposition held in Chicago in 1893, and Mrs. Candace Wheeler, director of the Woman's Building and exhibits. Mrs. Palmer founded the Needlework and Textile Guild at the Art Institute in Chicago, and Mrs. Wheeler, together with Louis Comfort Tiffany and his associates, established the Decorative Art Society in New York "to encourage profitable industries among women who possess artistic talent" and "to form classes in Art Needlework." Together with other craftsmen, Mrs. Wheeler also founded an organization called the Associated Artists, under whose direction important needlework commissions were undertaken.

In the 1890's, in Deerfield, Massachusetts, two painters, Margaret C. Whiting and Ellen Miller, established the Deerfield Blue and White Industry, thus fostering the first revival in the United States of an indigenous form of needlework at the local level. In keeping with the arts and crafts movement pioneered by William Morris in England, the two ladies made a study of old receipts for dyeing their flax threads with indigo or other vegetable dyes and adapted floral and vine motives from eighteenth-century embroideries which they found in the Connecticut River Valley.

In 1921, two years before her death, Candace Wheeler published the first book on *The Development of Embroidery in America*. Seventeen years later, Georgiana Brown Harbeson in *American Needlework* (1938) included in her historical survey over a hundred modern examples of her own work and that of contemporaries such as Mrs. Nicholas E. Brown of Newport and Mrs. Theodore Roosevelt, Jr. of New York.

One might suppose that during the next twenty years interest in needlework would have flagged. But not at all. In 1959 an important exhibition of New England Crewel Embroideries was held at the Connecticut Historical Society in response "to the constructive and active curiosity" of women concerned with restoring or decorating houses in the eighteenth- and early nineteenth-century style. At that time, Adolph S. Cavallo, then Assistant Curator of Textiles at the Museum of Fine Arts in Boston, wrote an outstanding article on the subject for the Society's *Bulletin*. Three years later, Gore Place, in Waltham, Massachusetts, was the site of another exhibition of crewelwork found in New England. In 1965, Barbara Gilbert, a Winterthur Fellow, completed, under my direction, a detailed study of dated and documented pieces of "American Crewelwork, 1700-1850" for her master's thesis at the University of Delaware. Although the exhibitions lasted but a short time, and the thesis has not yet been published, the research carried out in connection with them has contributed greatly to the knowledge of early American needlework and has led to the publication in the 1960's of no less than six books with particular emphasis on stitchery or "how-to-do-it." Among them is *American Crewelwork: Stitches of the Seventeenth and Eighteenth Centuries* (1962), the first work of the present

12   authors. Mary Taylor Landon and Susan Burrows Swan.

Mrs. Landon and Mrs. Swan, members of the Winterthur Museum guiding staff, have made a specialty of antique American needlework and have studied the embroideries in this museum and in other public and private collections. Mrs. Landon, who has concentrated on motifs and stitches, gives credit to The Women's Educational and Industrial Union in Boston for helping her to ascertain how particular stitches were worked. Her interest in stitchery parallels Mrs. Swan's study of the historical and design aspects of American embroidery. As a background for present-day designs, Mrs. Swan outlines women's interest in needlework during the past two centuries and defines various types. About 35 illustrations of old needlework in this section have not been published heretofore. Also fresh and new are their step-by-step drawings of 25 stitches most frequently found in New England embroideries with suggestions for suitably combining them to work flowers, leaves, animals, and birds.

More than knowledge of antique crewelwork and interest in how it was done make this an unusual manual. Mrs. Landon and Mrs. Swan not only wish to make it easy for women to learn how to do crewelwork the American way, but they also encourage women to be creative. They deplore the use of kits, often filled with poor materials and patterns, and advocate, instead, that needlewomen make their own selections of fine vegetable-dyed yarns and high-grade background materials. Toward this end, reliable suppliers (as well as designers) are listed. The authors heartily believe in the pleasure and satisfaction to be derived from original work skillfully executed.

FLORENCE M. MONTGOMERY
Assistant Curator (Textile)
The Henry Francis du Pont Winterthur Museum

I

HISTORICAL BACKGROUND

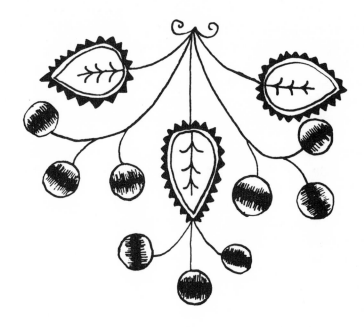

*I*t is difficult for us to imagine the significance of needlework in a colonial woman's life. A wife's needlework capability was an important economic factor to her family. It was essential that a woman know how to prepare yarn, fashion clothing, and maintain and repair, as well as execute, the decorative effects for the textiles in the home.

Women had few opportunities for self-expression and it was surely a satisfaction to receive praise and admiration for needlework. Even as late as 1805, when woman's role and education were broadened, a magazine article entitled "The Female Sex" said,

> While I am conscious of being an intelligent moral being; while I see myself denied, in so many cases, the exercise of my own discretion, incapable of separate property, subject in all periods of my life to the will of another, on whose bounty I am made to depend for food and shelter; when I see myself, in my relation to society, regarded merely as a beast, as an insect, passed over, in the distribution of public duties, as absolutely nothing . . . .[1]

A lady unskilled in the use of a needle was comparable to a gentleman who did not know how to use a sword. With the great amount of utility sewing and mending required for the home and family, it must have been pleasant to find time to decorate a few items.

In 1777, fourteen-year-old Nancy Shippen of Philadelphia received what was probably typical instruction from her mother: "Needle work is a most important branch of female education."[2] Nancy was from a prominent Philadelphia family and received schooling in other aspects considered necessary to her future life in society. Her mother's letter went on to say, ". . . tell me how you have improved in holding your head & sholders, in making a curtsy, in going out or coming into a room, in giving & receiving, holding your knife & fork, walking & seting. . . ." Imagine the stultifying effect on a young girl when these were considered the essentials of her education. Needlework provided one of the few challenges in her niche. No wonder careful attention was given to its instruction and execution.

Numerous advertisements to teach needlework appeared in the newspapers, often placed by widows or unmarried women. This was one of the few acceptable methods by which a woman could support herself. Mrs. Carroll, in the *New York Mercury* of 1765, said she "proposes teaching young ladies plain work, Samplars, French Quilting, knoting for Bed Quilts or Toilets, Dresden, flowering on Cat Gut, Shading (with Silk or Worsted on Cambrick, Lawn, or Holland)."[3] We no longer recognize many of the terms. "Dresden" meant drawn or pulled thread work, "cat gut" was canvas work, and "shadings with worsted" was crewelwork on one of several possible grades of linen.[4]

Another important fact which is hard for us to comprehend was the scarcity of cloth ornamented with printed or brocaded patterns. The prints and woven designs we take for granted today existed only in imported fabrics. The average family used solid-colored fabrics relieved by an occasional check. The most inexpensive way to add gay patterns to her home and clothes was for the colonist to embroider them herself. We should keep these factors in mind when we see the infinite amount of effort that went into these embroideries.

Although women contributed little except the textile arts to America's decorative arts, the total effect was significant.

Categories of Crewelwork

Before Shakespeare's time, the English word *crewel* meant slackly twisted, two-ply, worsted yarn. Worsted yarns are spun from long wool fibers carefully combed parallel before twisting. As with many other words, there was no standardized spelling for crewel and it appeared in numerous ways in old documents. It can be both puzzling and amusing to encounter spellings like crewell, crewle, cruel, croole, and croull.

Definition of the word *crewelwork* has always depended on the use of crewel yarns, and is not related to design, kind of stitches, or background fabric. Canvas work, Turkey work, and Berlin work also were done with two-ply worsted yarns and can be called crewelwork.

CREWEL EMBROIDERY

Wool embroidery has its own individual charm. By using the two most easily grown and processed fibers, wool and flax, our ancestors produced fabrics that not only wore well but added warmth to the home. Using these accessible and inexpensive materials and adding endless hours of labor, a housewife could create bright embroideries of graceful flowers and fanciful foliage to enliven even the plainest surroundings. Perhaps because of this labor of love, embroidery worked by a relative as opposed to that made by professionals was more apt to be saved for sentimental reasons. Only wear and the moth were (and are) crewelwork's major enemies. It owes part of its survival, especially in England, to its homey materials. More elegant forms, usually the work of professionals, included gold and silver threads, beads, and sequins. In times of stress or change of fashion, metal embroideries were frequently unraveled to be melted for the silver or gold content. This was a fashionable pastime called "drizzling."[5]

CANVAS WORK

What we call "needlepoint" today was known as "canvas work" until the early nineteenth century. Canvas work done on a background coarser than 8 squares to the linear inch should properly be called "gros point," and that on grounds finer than 16 to 18 squares per linear inch should be termed "petit point." Gros point is used for rugs and requires several strands of coarse yarns. Most of the work from the sixteenth through eighteenth centuries was done on fine grounds ranging from 20 to 45 holes to the inch. The finer the canvas and yarn the more intricate may be the design created. In Plate 45 the flame pattern of the old purse (44 holes to the inch) was enlarged on the new purse by using coarser canvas (24 holes to the inch). The background fabrics may be any evenly woven material—cotton, linen, wool or even silk.

Over fifty different canvas-work stitches are recognized today. The three most used during the sixteenth, seventeenth, and eighteenth centuries were Tent Stitch, done diagonally, Flame or Florentine, worked vertically, and Cross Stitch. (See Part II for instructions in stitches.) Occasionally, French Knots were added for accents.

Wool has always been the most popular filling, although silk yarn has also been used. Crewel yarns work well on petit point canvas and are very serviceable. Its great wearing qualities have made crewel canvas work more desirable than embroidered crewel for upholstery. Chairs surviving from the eighteenth century with their original canvas work attest to its merits.

BERLIN WORK

Berlin work was the creation of an early nineteenth-century printseller in Berlin named A. Philipson. His patterns and those of others who followed him were printed from engraved copper plates. Lines were ruled in the plates so that the printed patterns appeared to be drawn on squared paper. Hundreds of women were employed to hand color thousands of prints made during the nineteenth century. The pattern was stitched by exact transfer of the design, one square on paper for one square on canvas. To simplify the process, special canvas was woven about 1820 with blue threads to indicate every tenth stitch.

Most of this work in its early years was done with worsted crewel yarns. Later a softer, longer-fibered, less springy yarn was developed from Merino wool. Many contemporary references continued to call this work crewelwork until about 1840.

Berlin work was immensely popular from 1820 until 1870. It eclipsed most other forms of needlework during this period. Prevalent themes for Berlin work were biblical scenes, churches, historical events, dogs and cats, and large flowers massed together. In his typically acid style, Mark Twain described a Berlin work picture in a rivertown mansion in *Life on the Mississippi*:

> Over middle of mantel, engraving—"Washington Crossing the Delaware"; on the wall by the door, copy of it done in thunder-and-lightning crewels by one of the young ladies—work of art which would have made Washington hesitate about crossing, if he could have foreseen what advantage was going to be taken of it.

Berlin work was usually done 10 to 16 squares to the inch; Victorian women claimed that their eyes were too weak for more delicate work.

TURKEY WORK

Turkey work is mentioned frequently in inventories of the sixteenth and seventeenth centuries in England and in America until the mid-eighteenth century. The fabrics were intended primarily for upholstery and carpets. (*Carpets* referred to pieces used on tops of tables or cupboards rather than on floors.) Robert Feke's painting of the prominent Isaac Royall and his family, painted in 1741 and owned today by the Harvard Law School, includes a "true" Turkey carpet. Although adapted for a variety of patterns and styles, the term *Turkey work* probably originated from attempts to copy the design and manner of the exotic Turkish carpets.

In some Turkey work, woolen yarns were knotted on the warp threads of a loom. Then a coarse linen weft was shot across to hold these knots in place. This may not have been the only form of Turkey work. A more delicate type, perhaps using crewels, is mentioned in a Boston advertisement of 1716, "Turkey-Work for Handkerchiefs two ways."[6] The work was still being done in 1758, judging by an amusing letter a man wrote to the *New York Mercury* that year about the huge quantities of various types of needlework forced upon his daughters by his wife. He felt there should be time for them to learn to read and write! His comment was, "About a month ago, Tent and Turkey-stitch seemed at a stand; my Wife knew not what new Work to introduce. . . ."[7]

A stitch called Turkey work is still listed in some embroidery books. It is essentially a Back or Cross Stitch with the surface thread left raised in loops instead of being drawn down firmly. The loops can then be cut to create a fuzzy pile.

Unfortunately, few examples of Turkey work survive today; it is the least understood form of crewelwork. Fine canvas work and early Berlin work that also used crewel yarns are less appreciated than the best known and loved form of crewelwork, embroidery.

English Crewelwork

American crewelwork is based firmly on English needlework traditions, and it is appropriate, therefore, to consider the development of needlework in England.

FACTORS IN DEVELOPMENT

When Henry VIII broke with the Roman Catholic Church, he divided the great monastic holdings, thus distributing the lands to a larger segment of the population. With new wealth and opportunities, people who previously could not afford embroidery now began to imitate royalty by ornamenting their clothing and homes. Here begins the story of embroidery by and for the middle class in England. The professionals now found fewer of their patrons among the church and more from the aspiring new middle class. Embroidery for personal adornment reached its peak during the sixteenth century. Embroideries costing 50 pounds a yard embellished clothing for men and women who could afford such luxuries.

It is thought that steel needles were introduced to Europe by the Moors sometime in the fourteenth century. Prior to the mid-sixteenth century only bone needles or the European steel ones were available in England. The manufacture of English steel needles was sufficiently established by the mid-seventeenth century for a guild of needlemakers to be formed. Readily accessible fine English steel needles facilitated this new, broader interest in embroidery.

Household furnishings and architecture influenced the types and designs of embroidery. Before the late 1400's, beds were placed in halls, and curtains were hung from a large ring, chain, or rope in the ceiling to surround the bed. These curtains were drawn up during the day and released at night to ward off draughts. It was only during the late fifteenth century that separate rooms began to be set aside as bedrooms. Gradually, beds with posts to hold fabrics for privacy and warmth became popular. Massively turned posts with heavy fabrics for curtains were used in the sixteenth century by those who could afford them. Poor people had only pallets of straw.

The importance of the bed itself as a major piece of room furniture persisted until the nineteenth century. Royalty often received important guests in the bed chamber. Even in modest homes the finest fabric in the household was used on the master bed. The richness of fabric a family could display indicated its social and financial standing. It was sometimes customary among the wealthy and middle classes to drape the room in black fabrics at the time of mourning even if the fabrics were rented for that purpose.

Rooms had multiple uses, especially in smaller homes, and beds were found in most of them. Embroidered bed hangings were an ideal way to enliven the room and display a woman's skill. Complete sets of English hangings of crewel embroidery and canvas work survive in England and can be seen at the Victoria and Albert Museum in London. Several museums in this country including the Governor's Palace in Colonial Williamsburg and the Ashley House in Old Deerfield, Massachusetts, show elaborate English crewelwork bed hangings. Plate 1 shows a beautiful example in The Henry Francis du Pont Winterthur Museum and Plate 2 is an enlargement of a portion.

As additional, larger furniture forms evolved, they presented more surface to be decorated. Embroidery was a natural solution. During the sixteenth, seventeenth, and eighteenth centuries, loose chair cushions called "squabs" made board seats bearable. As upholstered furniture gradually appeared, it was customary to have window hangings, bed furnishings, and chair coverings all of the same material or pattern. One of the most interesting examples owned by the Victoria and Albert Museum shows crewel embroidery and canvas work with the same design and color scheme. Using the embroidered crewel for curtains and the more durable canvas work for chairbacks provided a practical way to maintain a unified pattern in a room.

With so many surfaces to be covered, it would have been impossible for a housewife to accomplish the task alone. A group of male professional embroiderers formed a guild which was granted its first charter as early as 1551. The Society of the Art and Mistery of the Broderers of the City of London or the Broderers Company, as it was called, established strict standards of workmanship and terms of apprenticeship. Before the completed work could be sold it had to be submitted to the Guild and meet its specifications, or be destroyed.

The Guild seems to have been especially active during the Elizabethan and Jacobean eras, producing embroidered clothing, bed and window hangings, screens, and even wall hangings. Work done by Guild members was usually more uniformly executed than that of the nonprofessional. It was also characteristically more elaborate in design. Each piece was worked with a variety of couched and interwoven stitches to create exotic floral and foliage effects. A typical example with large trees growing from a solidly stitched mound of earth is shown in Plate 3 with a detail illustration on Plate 4.

During the late seventeenth century, much more of the background fabric was covered with embroidery than in the eighteenth century. Broad expanses of intricate work possibly intimidated amateurs. The lighter designs of mid-eighteenth century probably had a greater appeal to the housewife because they were easier to embroider and required less time to finish a piece. The importance of the Broderers Guild appears to wane by the middle of the eighteenth century.

DESIGN SOURCES

Design sources for crewelwork were manifold. Some of the most useful were such illustrative materials as illuminated manuscripts, needlework pattern books, botany books, ornithology books, wallpapers, and engravings. Imported fabrics, particularly those from India and China, provided additional ideas.

Delicate scrolls, flowers, and fine leaves were elements of manuscript illumination. The Scriveners' Company created decorated devices for charters and other important documents as late as the seventeenth century. Most households contained at least one book, a Bible, with flowered letters at the heads of chapters.

Several of the early needlework pattern books printed in England were direct copies of even older German and Italian books. A popular English work, *A Schole-house for the Needle* by Richard Shorleyker, was published in 1624. Patterns with flowers and stems were stylized, frequently coiled to form repeating borders, but animals, insects, butterflies, fish, crabs and birds were drawn quite realistically. All were line drawings, without indications for shading or stitches to be employed.

Books such as Topsell's *Historie of four-footed beasts* (1606) and Moufet's *Insectorum* (1658) reflected the general interest in botany and biology prevalent during the seventeenth and eighteenth centuries in England. Books of this type were owned by the better educated and wealthier families who had more time for needlework. Even amateur adaptations from these books made charming embroidery designs.

English-made, hand-blocked wallpapers and lining papers were produced early in the seventeenth century. Most of these were in small panels and stressed floral motifs. Almost a century later, the English imported longer, hand-painted rolls from China that featured flowering trees with numerous birds darting between the branches. For those that could afford them, wallpapers provided inspirations for designs.

During the eighteenth century, popular engravings were traced, especially for canvas-work scenes. A book called the *Ladies' Amusement,* published in London in 1758-62, contained hundreds of flowers, birds, and bugs that were intended as patterns. Because motifs from this book were traced so often, only a few complete copies remain unmutilated.

INDIAN INFLUENCE

Much has been written about the influence of Indian fabrics upon English crewel designs. There is, however, sufficient evidence to suggest that there may have been a reciprocal influence of English design upon the Indian. John Irwin, Keeper, Indian Section, Victoria and Albert Museum, found that between 1615 and 1619 the English East India Company sent English embroidery *to* India as presents for Indian nobility.[8] Apparently these English fabrics delighted Indian Maharajahs, and their embroiderers busied themselves copying both the stitches and designs. Before Irwin's research the opposite influence had generally been considered the case. Later, Indian hand-painted cottons, called "palimpores," were sent to England, where they were used as bedspreads or wall hangings. These cottons had a large, so-called tree-of-life pattern. The Indians did not slavishly copy English patterns but added their own touches to the flowers, leaves, and branches. Although the Indians preferred colored backgrounds, at the request of English factors they left larger white background areas. In 1722, prompted by the wool industry, Parliament passed a law prohibiting the use of imported painted cottons in England. Until its repeal in 1774, embroidery may have provided an important means for most women to furnish their homes with the exotic flowers and foliage they had come to love.

Very fine Indian cottons with polychrome silk embroidery were also sent to England before 1722. Today we are astounded by the minute Chain Stitches with which these fabrics were worked. Some experts think the Chain Stitch originated in India. Painted designs, identical to the embroidered ones, have also been found; the same stencil was evidently used for both patterns.

24

CHINESE INFLUENCE

The Portuguese began regular trade with China after 1514, and a few prized Chinese silk embroideries came to England by way of Portugal. After 1600, when the British formed their own company to go directly to China, the importation of these fabrics increased. They were so popular in England that by 1701, to protect English textile industries, laws had to be passed forbidding the wearing or use of silks from China, Persia, or the East Indies.

The delicate Chinese silk embroideries seemingly done without regard for time or eyesight were an inspiration to English women. One of the major Chinese contributions to crewel designs was the fanciful, asymmetric, slanting trees rising from hummocks of earth. Exotic phoenix birds flitted through the embroidered leaves with open beaks. Many techniques were inspired by Chinese work. Subtle shading was obtained by the intricate use of Satin Stitch and Long-and-Short, which were similar. The accent or texture stitch popularly called French Knot possibly originated in China. It is sometimes referred to as the Peking Stitch.

Unfortunately, while contributing many beautiful aspects to crewelwork, Chinese silk embroideries also helped ultimately to outmode it. The lure of the more expensive, lustrous thread on glowing silk satin grounds overwhelmed crewelwork, making it seem shabby and dull.

MATERIALS USED

Fustian, the most common ground material for English crewelwork, was woven with a linen warp and a cotton weft in a twill weave. The linen warp provided strength while the cotton weft added softness. Occasionally, in the later eighteenth century, all-cotton fustian was used. Some was called tufted fustian and resembled today's corduroy.

Undoubtedly the greatest single influence on American crewelwork was its English foundation. But many individual factors blended to create English crewelwork: the rise of the middle class, the architecture and furniture styles, the Broderers Guild, Indian influences, and Chinese influences.

American Crewelwork

Little if any seventeenth-century crewelwork can be positively identified as American. The earliest documented American examples that survive date from the early eighteenth century. Contemporary documents, however, confirm that crewelwork was done here in the seventeenth century. In 1687, Mr. Samuel Sewall asked a friend in London to send him white fustian marked with designs to embroider bed hangings and a half dozen chairs, together with enough worsted to do the work.[9] A subsequent letter mentioned that his two young daughters were about to enter school and his wife wanted this work to keep them from idleness. A New Haven estate of Governor Theophelus Eaton in 1656 listed six cushions of Turkey work, two of needlework, a great chair of needlework, and "cruells" and "canvis."[10]

During the seventeenth century, most women were kept busy providing the necessities of life and had little time to make decorative embroideries for themselves or their homes. The first nonutilitarian pieces of needlework attempted were probably samplers worked with silk thread on linen grounds. The few surviving seventeenth-century samplers are long and narrow. In England and in America, samplers served to record intricate patterns and techniques for mature seamstresses. These samplers frequently had designs arrayed in horizontal rows and were like notebooks of stitches. In the eighteenth century, samplers were the initial sewing efforts by girls of six to fifteen years of age. By that time samplers had become squarer and were primarily pictorial with borders surrounding verses. Fewer types of stitches were used at this time, with the Cross Stitch dominating.

DESIGN SOURCES

Some women surely must have brought pieces of family crewelwork with them from England. If the woman lived in an isolated area these British examples doubtless became primary sources for design and stitch reference.

A specific instance of women sending to England for linen with designs already drawn on it has been mentioned. Several contemporary local advertisements mentioned complete bed furniture designs together with other pieces such as chair coverings or curtains for windows.[11] Whenever possible it seems to have been the custom here as well as in England to do the whole room in the same material and design.

Several teachers proudly state that they were "lately from" London.[12] Needlework done in America with English yarns, on English linen, according to English patterns in stitches learned from British teachers would be difficult to distinguish from crewel done in England. Such work exists and leads to much controversy. Any variation in elements provides hope for discovering its true identity.

As in this century many women sought professional help for drawing an outline of the design. Numerous eighteenth-century advertisements offered designs drawn on linen or canvas, sometimes slyly adding that it would be cheaper than the work from London.[13] Certainly elements of these patterns once purchased were traced, passed around, and used again and again. The example shown in Plates 17 and 18 is closely related in design to hangings owned by The Shelburne Museum in Vermont.

26   Several short-lived magazines, for example, *Gentlemen and Lady's Town*

and Country Magazine, printed in Boston in 1784, and *Lady's Magazine,* printed in Philadelphia in 1792, published articles that attempted to appeal to women. More successful ones like Rudolph Ackermann's *The Repository of Arts,* printed in London beginning in 1809, and *The Lady's Book,* printed in Philadelphia beginning in 1830, published patterns and instructions for needlework. With these printed patterns available in magazines, women were less dependent upon professional designers and teachers than they had been in the eighteenth century.

Many small schools of needlework, often run by a widow or a spinster, were established in America during the eighteenth century. The teacher provided designs and probably had her own individual approach to elements and subjects. Consequently, one could probably have recognized many items as having been done under the direction of individual teachers or in certain schools, which may account for the similarity in many subjects surviving today. If girls lived in the country or at a distance, they were sent to board at the school or with relatives in town. Each school's sphere of influence was expanded when a girl returned to her home area and demonstrated her new embroidery techniques and designs to her sisters and friends.

Popular engravings were traced or copied to provide some crewel designs. In 1790, James Cox of Philadelphia advertised in the *Pennsylvania Packet* that he would accurately copy copperplate prints, maps, and paintings for needlework.[14] Two popular themes, the shepherdess (Plate 5) and the fishing lady, we believe were copied or traced from English prints. Although at least 65 needlework copies have been preserved, the prints from which they were derived have not yet been found.

The best evidence for the conclusion that some women drew their own designs is found in advertisements offering instruction in drawing. Typical is one by Peter Hall, upholsterer, in Chestnut Street, Philadelphia, dated 1745. In addition to making all kinds of furniture, this versatile man offered to "teach any Person to draw Draughts in a short Time for Flourishing or Embroidering at the most reasonable Rates."[15]

Surely many women who drew charmingly naive and fanciful designs never received any formal instruction. Simply by adding imaginative scrolls and attenuated lines to drawings of flowers seen in her own garden the embroiderer created lovely designs. Most of the hills, trees, fruits, and animals found in American crewelwork were the familiar sights of her small world. A few of the birds are even drawn and shaded accurately enough to be recognized as particular species today.

The Lady's Book, first published by L. A. Godey & Co. in 1830, stated that "... subjects drawn and coloured on the holland, or silk, may be purchased at many of the fancy shops,"[16] which suggests that at least by 1830 patterns for crewel included indications of colors. The writer advised that, "it is only necessary to follow, as closely as possible, the colouring and shading of the artist in the ground sketch, and good taste will avail more than a volume of instructions." On none of the old crewelwork examined by the authors have suggestions for coloring on the linen been found. We hope this idea only applied to a few of the later examples. With so little left to the creative imagination, the needleworker would feel less involved. In any case, crewel was almost completely replaced by other needle arts by 1830.

PROFESSIONAL MALE EMBROIDERERS

It has not been widely recognized that professional male embroiderers worked in the colonies. Although there may have been only a few here, advertisements in Boston, New York, and Philadelphia attest that at least six men offered their services as professional embroiderers.[17] Two also boasted the additional skill of dry cleaning. An advertisement in the *New York Gazette* of November 6, 1758 said:

> Levy Simons, Embroiderer from London, informs the Ladies and Gentlemen, That, besides Gold and Silver, he works in Silk and Worsted, Shading; likewise Robins and Facings, Shoes &c. He Cleans Gold and Silver lace, takes Spots out of Silk and Cloths, &c. &c. to be heard of at I. Abrahams, near the Kings Arms.[18]

So far there is no evidence that a guild of embroiderers operated in this country. A Mr. Buriat, however, advertised for apprentices in Philadelphia in 1794.[19] Probably most came to this country fully trained and continued to follow their professions. The mere presence of such professionals would have established a level of workmanship to emulate.

Several men advertised that they would teach embroidery, draw designs, or teach others to do so. One of these, Peter Pelham of Boston, was the stepfather of John Singleton Copley, foremost of our American artists. It certainly seems an appropriate male occupation in a day when more embroidery was lavished on men's apparel than on women's.

AMERICAN HOMES AND FURNITURE

The style of American furniture in vogue certainly influenced designs of the embroidery done for it. Heavy, massive flowers and leaves were appropriate for seventeenth-century and William and Mary chairs and beds. Smaller flowers and animals suited the delicate curvilinear style of Queen Anne introduced about 1725. During the Chippendale period, approximately 1755-1785, a more vigorous and elaborate rococo ornament entered. Small motifs, bouquets, and vases of flowers became popular toward the end of the eighteenth century to accompany the classical grace of the Federal period.

Typical seventeenth-century houses were small, often only a single room to a floor. Families were large, and multipurpose rooms became a necessity even in a four-room house. The master bed was frequently in the parlor until the middle of the eighteenth century.

Inventories made after the death of a householder provide one of our best sources of information about home furnishings. The sparseness of furnishings of middle-class homes listed in inventories up to the mid-eighteenth century is striking to us today. Beds, joint stools, a few chairs, a table, possibly a cupboard, and a looking glass are found in the average inventory. Household linens were usually listed separately.

Until about 1740, Turkey work is sometimes mentioned specifically for upholstery, cushions, and carpets. Unfortunately, items are more often refered to as *wrot*. Judgment of whether this means Turkey work, canvas work, crewel or silk embroidery can only be made on the basis of existing examples and change of fashion. Rarely do inventories list window hangings. We know of no examples of seventeenth-century window hangings which can be positively identified. Carpets for the floor were very expensive and are seldom mentioned. Skins were the most commonly used floor covering in most homes. *Ruggs* referred more often to bed or table coverings, that is, coarsely embroidered or hooked blankets used on beds or tables. Beds and every item ·of their "furniture" were usually listed first and had the highest value in most of these early inventories. A bed furnishing listed in an inventory from Boston in 1735 was noted as "In Great Chamber 1 wrot. Curtains, Valens, Bass Mouldings Raised head cornishes Bedstead and curtain Rods—15 pounds."[20] Another chamber bed that must have been attractive was owned by Peter Faneuil of Boston: "hangings embroidered fustian curtains lined with green damask."[21] Without specific mention it is safer to assume that the "curtains" mentioned were for beds rather than windows.

Half tester, half headed, or press beds were all eighteenth-century terms for a folding bed (Plate 6). They provided a practical and attractive arrangement to enlarge the floor space of a room. When the bed was folded up, side curtains, often projecting from a frame attached to the bed or the ceiling, could be drawn around to mask it. What an enticing area for needlework! Unfortunately, few of these beds survive, and none with its original crewel hangings.

In the seventeenth century, a prosperous family's prized possessions of silver or delftware were displayed on a court or livery cupboard, the top of which was usually covered with a cloth. Because they did not present too formidable an expanse to cover, the embroidering of cupboard cloths probably appealed to the busy housewife. Similar cloths were laid on tables, and at mealtime they were covered with linen tablecloths to protect them.

During the second quarter of the eighteenth century, a variety of furniture forms—easy chairs, tea tables, and sofas—evolved. Refinements such as silver, glass, and ceramics, usually imported from England, were introduced into the home, revealing a more affluent, gracious life.

Most of the beautiful examples of crewel embroidery that we admire today were worked in the period from 1725 to 1825. Increased mention of crewel is noticed in diaries and wills during this period. Newspapers, too, have more advertisements for supplies and instructions at this time. Canvas, shaded crewels, silk yarns, and even gold and silver threads for embroidery were regularly advertised in the newspapers, particularly in the larger cities of Boston, New York, and Philadelphia.

REGIONAL PREFERENCES

Only a few distinctions can be drawn about regional preferences in American crewel embroidery. The previously mentioned fishing lady and shepherdess themes seemed to have been favored in the area around Boston; some scenes of this type are done in canvas work (Plate 7) and some in crewel embroidery (Plates 8 and 9). Even when the woman was not actually portrayed, nearly identical motifs of hills, trees, and animals appear, particularly on petticoat bands. An advertisement of 1749 describes such a petticoat:

> On the 11th of Nov. last, was stolen out of the Yard of Mr. Joseph Coit, Joiner in Boston, living in Cross Street, a Woman's Fustian Petticoat, with a large work'd Embroider'd Border, being Deer, Sheep, Houses, Forrest, &c., so worked. Whoever has taken the said Petticoat, will return it to the Owner thereof, or to the Printer, shall have 40s. old Tenor Reward and no Question ask'd.[22]

In the Connecticut River Valley there was a strong trend toward very large, bold flowers attached to broad stems with subsidiary patterns within their outlines. Sometimes these interior designs resemble shaded scales or are filled with flowers and vines (Color Plate I).

Although today the interest in crewel embroidery has spread to most areas of our country, it does not seem to have been equally popular in all the colonies during the seventeenth and eighteenth centuries. In an endeavor to distinguish regional differences during the period from the late seventeenth century through the early nineteenth century, newspapers, wills, inventories, diaries, and letters of Boston, Hartford, Providence, New York, Philadelphia, Baltimore, and Charleston were searched. Needlework mate-

30

rials, equipment, and instructors were cited with far less frequency south of Connecticut. A small amount of crewel embroidery apparently was done in Pennsylvania.

At the present time no known example of eighteenth-century crewel embroidery originating south of Maryland exists. In warmer climates women may have found it uncomfortable to work with woolen yarns and this may explain the scarcity of southern examples. Moreover, the warm effect in the home of the bright, woolen embroideries was an advantage in the colder climates of New England, whereas, in the warmer areas this effect was less appealing. Canvas work, on the other hand, seems to have been about equally prevalent in the northern and middle colonies, perhaps because the quality gave it a utilitarian value outweighing the purely decorative embroidery.

SEWING TOOLS

Today we take sewing implements for granted and it is hard to appreciate how treasured they were. A thimble was a prized possession and a popular gift. Thimbles made of brass were common, but they were also made of ivory, bone, silver, and occasionally gold. The gold thimble Paul Revere made for his youngest daughter, Maria, can be seen today in the Museum of Fine Arts in Boston. Cases to hold and protect thimbles were made of silver, bone, wood, tortoise shell, and enamel.

Needles were expensive and usually imported into the colonies. As early as 1742, however, an advertisement in a Boston newspaper stated that Simon Smith made and sold white Chapple Needles and all other kinds round and square.[23] In 1765, a New York firm that sold fish hooks and needles made in Pennsylvania offered two good reasons to buy their needles:

> They are equal if not superior in Quality to any imported from Europe; and always free from Rust, which by the frequent Damps in Vessels, European made are always liable to. As that laudable Disposition of encouraging Our American Manufactories, so much abounds in this Province, the Maker flatters himself of the Merchants here, favouring him with their Orders . . . .[24]

Precious needles were carefully stored in lovely containers of silver, wood, tortoise shell, beadwork, and enamel work.

We think of "pin money" as a trifle, but to the early housewife pins were a luxury that cost the equivalent of five to ten cents apiece. In the eighteenth century they were made by hand of two pieces of metal wire. The heads were tiny coils, pounded to the shaft, then tinned all over. Pincushions with these handmade pins were popular and costly presents for an expectant mother or a new baby. Anna Green Winslow describes one of these presents in her diary:

31

My aunt stuck a white sattan pincushin for Mrs. Waters. On one side, is a planthorn with flowers, on the reverse, just under the border are, on one side stuck these words, Josiah Waters, then follows on the end, Decr 1771, on the next side & end are the words, Welcome Little Stranger.[25]

Even today an occasional pincushion turns up with many of the pins still in place. Returning the pins to the original pattern not only taught patience but helped to discover strayed pins.

Most needlewomen used some form of stretching frame or hoop for embroidery to prevent puckering. Canvas work could stretch badly out of shape, particularly if done with the Tent Stitch, unless a frame was used. All sorts of hoops were made, ones to be held in the hand, to fasten to a table, or to stand on the floor. The one shown on Plate 10 was more elegant than most.

Ink was used to draw the design on the fabric. Perhaps this was called marking liquid, which one advertisement bragged would withstand washing on silk, cotton, and linen.[26] Sometimes the ink has oxidized and rotted the fibers of the ground cloth, causing the embroidery to be loosened. Occasionally, as in Plate 11, the work was not completed and the inked pattern shows clearly. The design was put on by a competent artist and seems to have been drawn directly on the fabric. Written references state that some designs were traced by a pricking wheel, and nutmeg or soot was rubbed in the holes.

PAPER VALANCES

An unusual item reflecting eighteenth-century crewel embroidery tastes is the paper valance. The Henry Francis du Pont Winterthur Museum owns three pieces probably used as bed valances and made of lightweight cardboard. The three pieces, two long side pieces and a shorter one for the end are completely shaped with scrolled ears at each end. Lovely crewel-type flowers, leaves, and a few birds are outlined in ink and lightly colored by watercolor washes. They may have been intended as a pattern to be traced; however, no evidence of tracing or pricking shows. It is unlikely that three valances with the same motifs would have been drawn and colored in detail if they were intended as patterns. Additional evidence for this practical short-cut appears in a 1794 advertisement from Charleston, South Carolina: "He also makes and sells bed and window cornishes, covered with colored paper, in the neatest and most elegant taste...."[27] Sometimes valances were also made of flowered wallpaper lined with newspaper.

CANVAS WORK

Today, typical canvas found for sale at needlework counters in department stores has the central motifs completed leaving the monotonous chore

COLOR PLATE I   *Bedspread, New England, 18th century.*
   American Crewel Embroidery

MATERIALS: Wool on linen

COLORS: Rust, four shades of blue, four shades of rose, three shades of
   gold crewel yarn

STITCHES: Roumanian Couching, Flat, Bullion, Buttonhole, Seed, Outline, Ladder, Weaving, and Lazy Daisy or Single Chain

Photograph by Charles P. Mills & Son
Courtesy The Henry Francis du Pont Winterthur Museum

PLATE 1 *Bed Hangings.*

   Worked by English professionals, probably Broderers Co.

MATERIALS: Wool and silk on fustian

COLORS: Four shades of peacock blue, three shades of indigo blue, three
   shades of rose, four shades of brown, four shades of green, and black,
   in silk thread and crewel yarn

STITCHES: Chain, Long-and-Short Buttonhole, Satin, Outline, and
   Ladder

HISTORY OF OWNERSHIP: In the William Penn family

Photograph by Gilbert Ask
Courtesy The Henry Francis du Pont Winterthur Museum

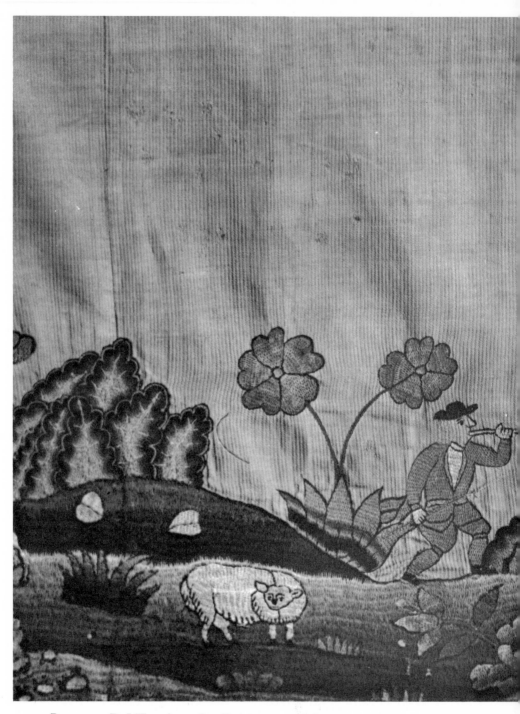

PLATE 2 *Bed Hangings, detail.*
Worked by English professionals, probably Broderers Co.

MATERIALS: Wool on fustian
COLORS: Four shades of peacock blue, four shades of brown, three shades
of indigo blue, two shades of green, and black crewel yarn

34

STITCHES: Long-and-Short Buttonhole, Satin, Outline
HISTORY OF OWNERSHIP: In the William Penn family

Photograph by Gilbert Ask
Courtesy The Henry Francis du Pont Winterthur Museum

35

PLATE 3 *Curtain.*

English Crewel Embroidery

MATERIALS: Wool on fustian

STITCHES: Long-and-Short Buttonhole, Satin, Weaving, Outline, French Knot, Squared Filling

Photograph by E. Irving Blomstrann
Courtesy Wadsworth Atheneum, Hartford, William B. Goodman Bequest

36

PLATE 4   *Curtain, detail from Plate 3.*
  English Crewel Embroidery

MATERIALS: Wool on fustian

STITCHES: Long-and-Short Buttonhole, Satin, Weaving, Outline, French
  Knot, Squared Filling

Photograph by E. Irving Blomstrann
Courtesy Wadsworth Atheneum, Hartford, William B. Goodman Bequest   37

PLATE 5 *Shepherdess.*
Worked by Temperance Parker. American Canvas Work

MATERIALS: Wool on canvas
COLORS: Peacock blue, white, black, gold, three shades of rose, and three
    shades of chocolate brown crewel yarn
STITCHES: Tent and French Knot

Photograph by Gilbert Ask
Courtesy The Henry Francis du Pont Winterthur Museum

38

PLATE 6   *Bed Furnishings for Folding Bed, New England.*
   American Crewel Embroidery

MATERIALS: Wool on linen

COLORS: Gold, shades of pink, shades of blue, and shades of green crewel
   yarn

STITCHES: Outline, Seed, Roumanian Couching, Satin, and Ladder

Photograph by Gilbert Ask
Courtesy The Henry Francis du Pont Winterthur Museum

PLATE 7 *Picture: Dog, Butterfly and Deer.*
American Canvas Work

MATERIALS: Wool on canvas
COLORS: Three shades of blue, three shades of peacock blue, two shades
of pink, beige, and four shades of brown crewel yarn
STITCH: Tent

Photograph by Gilbert Ask
Courtesy The Henry Francis du Pont Winterthur Museum

40

PLATE 8 *Picture.*
American Crewel Embroidery

MATERIALS: Silk and wool on linen
COLORS: Peacock blue, four shades of rose, sky blue, tan, beige, yellow,
white, and black crewel yarn
STITCHES: Roumanian Couching, Outline, Satin, Seed, and French Knot

Photograph by Gilbert Ask
Courtesy The Henry Francis du Pont Winterthur Museum

41

PLATE 9 *Picture.*
  American Crewel Embroidery

MATERIALS: Wool on linen
COLORS: Grey-blue, three shades of peacock blue, green, olive brown,
  gold, and three shades of rose crewel yarn
STITCHES: French Knot, Outline, and Roumanian Couching

Photograph by Gilbert Ask
Courtesy The Henry Francis du Pont Winterthur Museum

42

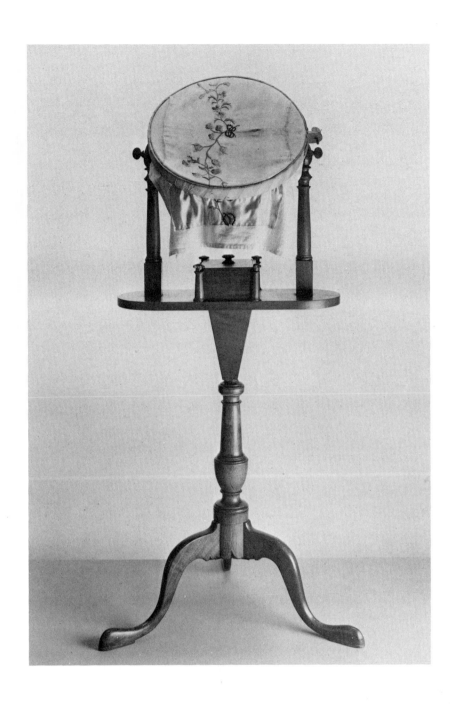

PLATE 10   *Embroidery Stand, American, 1785-95.*

MATERIALS: Mahogany

DESCRIPTION: Tripod base, snake feet, urn shaft, oval stand with slide-
topped compartment, round embroidery frame

Photograph by Gilbert Ask
Courtesy The Henry Francis du Pont Winterthur Museum   43

PLATE 11 *Petticoat Border, unfinished, detail.*
  American Crewel Embroidery

MATERIALS: Wool on linen
COLORS: Three shades of blue, beige, gold, rust, three shades of coral,
  three shades of rose, and three shades of green crewel yarn
STITCHES: Roumanian Couching, Outline, French Knot, and Seed
PATTERN: drawn in ink, unfinished

Photograph by Charles P. Mills & Son
Courtesy The Henry Francis du Pont Winterthur Museum

PLATE 12 *Queen Anne Chair Covering, original cover, Philadelphia.*
Outside arms and back are not covered in needlework. American Canvas Work

MATERIALS: Wool on canvas
COLORS: Tan, gold, black, green, two shades of blue, and three shades
of rose crewel yarn
STITCH: Florentine (up 4, back 2)

Photograph by Charles P. Mills & Son
Courtesy The Henry Francis du Pont Winterthur Museum

PLATE 13 *Table Cloth.*

"Mary Oothoyt, Her Table Cloth, This September the 9, 1759."
American Canvas Work

MATERIALS: Wool on canvas
COLORS: Three shades each of peacock blue, gold, and rose crewel yarn
STITCHES: Vertical or Florentine, and variations of the Cross Stitch

Photograph by Gilbert Ask
Courtesy The Henry Francis du Pont Winterthur Museum

PLATE 14   *Bed Furnishings, New York.*
   American Crewel Embroidery

MATERIALS: Wool on linen

COLORS: Three shades of indigo blue crewel yarn

STITCHES: Roumanian Couching, Outline, Flat, Seed, and Trellis
   Couching

Photograph by Gilbert Ask
Courtesy The Henry Francis du Pont Winterthur Museum

47

PLATE 15   **Bedspread.**
     American Crewel Embroidery
MATERIALS: Wool on linen
COLORS: Four shades of indigo crewel yarn
STITCHES: Roumanian Couching, Outline, Seed, Ladder, Satin, Back
   Flat, and variations of the Cross Stitch

Photograph by Gilbert Ask
Courtesy The Henry Francis du Pont Winterthur Museum

COLOR PLATE II *Bedspread, 1725-50.*
American Crewel Embroidery

MATERIALS: Wool on linen

COLORS: White, pink to rose, beige, three shades of blue, three shades of gold, and three shades of green crewel yarn

STITCHES: Roumanian Couching, Flat, Ladder, Outline, Satin, French Knot, Seed, and Bullion

Photograph by Charles P. Mills & Son
Courtesy The Henry Francis du Pont Winterthur Museum

PLATE 16 *Bedspread, 18th century.*
  American Crewel Embroidery

MATERIALS: Wool on twill-weave cotton
COLORS: Three shades of indigo blue crewel yarn
STITCHES: Outline, Roumanian Couching, Satin, and Chain
HISTORY OF OWNERSHIP: In the Hasbrouck family of New York

Photograph by Gilbert Ask
Courtesy The Henry Francis du Pont Winterthur Museum

49

PLATES 17 AND 18 *Bed Curtains.*
American Crewel Embroidery

MATERIALS: Wool on linen

COLORS: Mauve, yellow, shades of gold, shades of olive green, three
shades of grass green, three shades of pink to red, four shades of blue,
three shades of brown crewel yarn

50

STITCHES: Roumanian Couching, Weaving, Outline, Flat, Ladder, Spaced Buttonhole, Satin, and Bullion

Photograph by Gilbert Ask
Courtesy The Henry Francis du Pont Winterthur Museum

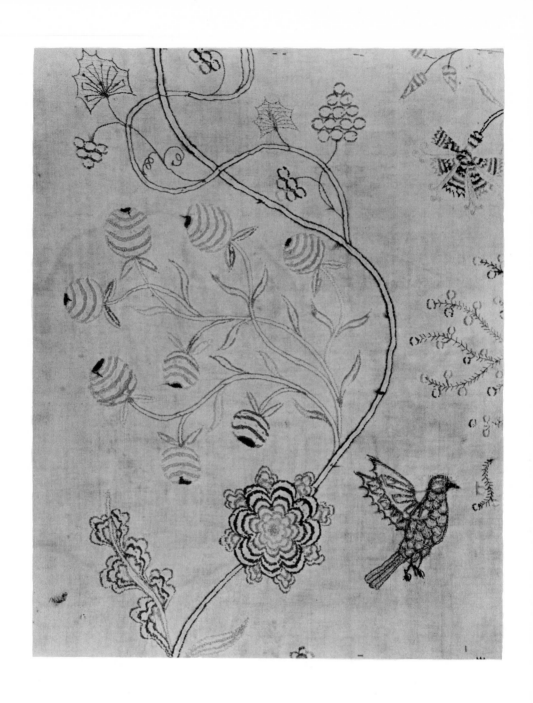

PLATE 19 *Bed Curtain, detail from back of bed curtain, Plate 18.*
American Crewel Embroidery

Photograph by Charles P. Mills & Son
Courtesy The Henry Francis du Pont Winterthur Museum

PLATE 20   *Bed Curtain, detail from front of bed curtain, Plate 18.*
   American Crewel Embroidery

MATERIALS: Wool on linen

COLORS: Peacock blue, grey blue, olive green, grass green, rose red, and shades of gold crewel yarn

STITCHES: Roumanian Couching, Bullion, Flat, Ladder, Outline, Weaving, and Back Stitch

Photograph by Charles P. Mills & Son
Courtesy The Henry Francis du Pont Winterthur Museum

PLATE 21 *Bed Furnishings, New England, 1760-70.*
   American Crewel Embroidery

MATERIALS: Wool on linen
COLORS: Shades of yellow, blue, green, mauve, gold, and rose pink crewel yarn
STITCHES: Roumanian Couching, Flat, Seed, Weaving, and Outline

Photograph by Gilbert Ask
Courtesy The Henry Francis du Pont Winterthur Museum

PLATE 22 *Coverlet, length 8', width 6½', 18th century.*
Probably worked by Lucinda Coleman. American Crewel Embroidery

MATERIALS: Wool on linen

COLORS: Center ground in shades of pink, brown, yellow, blue, gray, black, and occasional touches of green; borders in shades of blue crewel yarn

STITCHES: Roumanian Couching, Bullion, Outline, Weaving, and Flat

The Metropolitan Museum of Art, Sansbury-Mills Fund, 1961

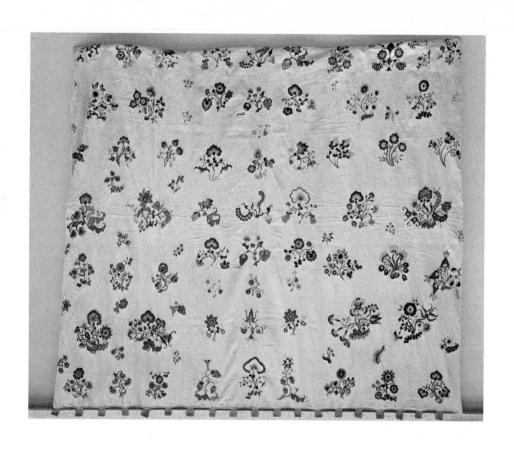

PLATE 23 *Bed Hangings, length 8', width 7'1", 18th century.*
Probably worked by Lucinda Coleman. American Crewel Embroidery

MATERIALS: Wool on linen
COLORS: Shades of light and dark blue, and black crewel yarn
STITCHES: Roumanian Couching, Bullion, Outline, Weaving, and Flat

The Metropolitan Museum of Art, Sansbury-Mills Fund, 1961

PLATE 24   *Chair Seat.*
   American Crewel Embroidery

MATERIALS: Wool, silk thread, and beads on linen
COLORS: Peacock blue, brown, tan, green, and rose to red crewel yarn
STITCHES: Roumanian Couching, Flat, Outline, and Weaving

Photograph by Charles P. Mills & Son
Courtesy The Henry Francis du Pont Winterthur Museum

PLATE 25   *Child's Dress.*
            American Crewel Embroidery

MATERIALS: Wool on linen
COLORS: Blue, rose, gold, and green crewel yarn
STITCHES: Flat and Outline

Photograph by Gilbert Ask
Courtesy The Henry Francis du Pont Winterthur Museum

58

PLATE 26 *Small Wool Blanket, 18th century.*
New England Christening Blanket, 41 1/2" long x 29 1/4" wide.
American Crewel Embroidery

MATERIALS: Wool on wool
COLORS: Three shades of indigo blue crewel yarn
STITCHES: Roumanian Couching, Outline, and Cross Stitch

Photograph by Gilbert Ask
Courtesy The Henry Francis du Pont Winterthur Museum

59

PLATE 27 *Petticoat Border.*
American Crewel Embroidery

MATERIALS: Wool on linen
COLORS: Dark blue, white, black, shades of peacock blue, shades of beige
to brown, and three shades of rose crewel yarn
STITCHES: Roumanian Couching, Outline, Fishbone, French Knot, and
Satin

Photograph by Gilbert Ask
Courtesy The Henry Francis du Pont Winterthur Museum

PLATE 28 *Double Pocket, mid-18th century.*
American or English Crewel Embroidery

MATERIALS: Wool on cotton broadcloth, lined with twill-weave cotton
COLORS: Shades of rose, brown, blue, yellow, and green crewel yarn
STITCHES: Chain, Bullion, Satin, and Back.
HISTORY OF OWNERSHIP: In the Gordon family, York, Pa.

Photograph by Gilbert Ask
Courtesy The Henry Francis du Pont Winterthur Museum

PLATE 29   *Man's Pocketbook, 1770.*

> *Inscribed: "When this you see, remember me.   Holder Slocy His Pocket-*
> *book 1770." American Canvas Work*

MATERIALS: Wool on canvas

COLORS: Coral, olive green, gold, and olive brown crewel yarn

STITCH: Vertical or Florentine

Photograph by Gilbert Ask
Courtesy The Henry Francis du Pont Winterthur Museum

61

PLATE 30 *Man's Pocketbook.*
    American Crewel Embroidery

MATERIALS: Wool on linen, with silver clasp
COLORS: Blue, two shades of rose, two shades of yellow, and black crewel
    yarn
STITCHES: Outline, Bullion, and Roumanian Couching

Photograph by Gilbert Ask
Courtesy The Henry Francis du Pont Winterthur Museum

62

PLATE 31 *Pot Holder.*
       American Crewel Embroidery

MATERIALS: Wool on cotton dimity
COLORS: Pink, blue, and black crewel yarn
STITCHES: Satin, Outline, Flat, and Chain

Photograph by Gilbert Ask
Courtesy The Henry Francis du Pont Winterthur Museum

PLATE 32 *Hand Firescreen.*
American Canvas Work

MATERIALS: Wool on canvas
COLORS: Three shades of rose, three shades of peacock blue, three shades
  of yellow, and black crewel yarn
STITCH: Tent

Photograph by Gilbert Ask
Courtesy The Henry Francis du Pont Winterthur Museum

64

PLATE 33 *Firescreen.*

> *Inscribed: "This work in hands my friends may have when I am dead and laid in grave and all my bones is rotten this you see to remember me that I am not forgotten Tanneke Pears her work done in New York year 1766." American Canvas Work*

MATERIALS: Wool on canvas, double mesh

COLORS: Three shades of peacock blue, three shades of gold, and two shades of rose crewel yarn

STITCHES: Tent and Florentine

Photograph by Gilbert Ask
Courtesy The Henry Francis du Pont Winterthur Museum

65

PLATE 34   *Sampler, "Anne King Her Sampler 1769."*
   American Canvas Work

MATERIALS: Wool on canvas

COLORS: brown, black, peacock blue, two shades of blue, and two shades
   of pink crewel yarn

STITCH: Tent

66

Photograph by Gilbert Ask
Courtesy The Henry Francis du Pont Winterthur Museum

PLATE 35 *Chair Seat, partially worked.*
Designed by Susan Swan. Worked by Mary Taylor Landon

MATERIALS: Wool on twill-weave linen
COLORS: Black and five shades each of olive green, olive brown, flame
red, and marine blue crewel yarn
STITCHES: Flat, Roumanian Couching, Fishbone, Outline, and Chain

Photograph by Edward T. Howell

PLATE 36 *Chair Seat.*

Designed by Susan Swan. Worked by Mary Taylor Landon

MATERIALS: Wool on twill-weave linen

COLORS: Five shades each of marine blue, flame red, olive green, and olive brown crewel yarn

STITCHES: Flat, Roumanian Couching, Outline, Seed, Ladder, Single Chain, Trellis Couching, and Wheel Buttonhole

68   *Photograph by Edward T. Howell*

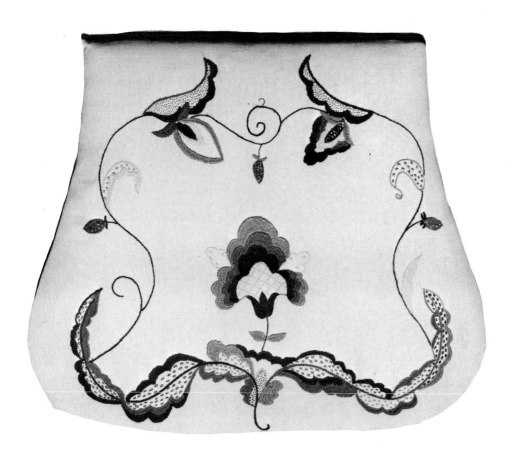

PLATE 37 *Chair Seat.*
  Designed by Susan Swan. Worked by Mary Taylor Landon

MATERIALS: Wool on twill-weave linen

COLORS: Four shades of blue crewel yarn

STITCHES: Roumanian Couching, Flat, Outline, Ladder, Satin, Cross, Single Chain, Seed, and Fishbone

Photograph by Edward T. Howell

69

PLATE 38 *Easy Chair.*

Designed by Susan Swan. Worked by Mrs. Robert A. Ramsdell

MATERIALS: Wool on twill-weave linen
COLORS: White and four shades of blue crewel yarn
STITCHES: Roumanian Couching, French Knot, Outline, Weaving, Trellis Couching, and Ladder

Photograph by Edward T. Howell

PLATE 39 *Sweaters.*

Left: Designed by Susan Swan. Worked by Mrs. Frederick A. Bowdle

MATERIALS: Wool on wool

COLORS: Beige, white, and two shades each of blue, green, rose, and yellow crewel yarn

STITCHES: French Knot, Chain, Fishbone, Ladder, Flat, and Long-and-Short Buttonhole

Center: Designed and worked by Mrs. Frederick A. Bowdle

COLORS: Elephant—bright blue with dark blue outlines. Butterfly—two shades each of bright green and pale orange crewel yarn

STITCHES: Chain, Ladder, Outline, Satin, and Flat

Right: Designed and worked by Mrs. Roger S. Bixby

COLORS: Shades of yellow, shades of green, and black crewel yarn

STITCHES: Flat, Satin, and Outline

Photograph by Edward T. Howell

71

PLATE 40 *Sweater.*

   Designed by Susan Swan. Worked by Mrs. E. Rogers Pleasants

MATERIALS: Wool on wool

COLORS: Shades of green, brown, and coral crewel yarn

STITCHES: Wheel Buttonhole, Flat, Roumanian Couching, Outline,
   French Knot, and Arrowhead

72   *Photograph by Edward T. Howell*

PLATE 41   *Pillow.*

> *Designed by Women's Educational and Industrial Union, Boston.*
> *Worked by Mary Taylor Landon*

MATERIALS: Wool on canvas

COLORS: Four shades each of rose, yellow, and blue, and five shades of green crewel yarn

STITCHES: Florentine (2 up, 1 down), 2 strands of crewel yarn on canvas 16 squares to the inch

Photograph by Edward T. Howell

PLATE 42   *Pillows, Three Companion Designs.*
Designed by Susan Swan. Worked by Mary Taylor Landon

MATERIALS: Wool on linen

COLORS: Four shades of bright rose, four shades of marine blue, three shades of grey green, and three shades of yellow crewel yarn

STITCHES: Roumanian Couching, Flat, Ladder, Outline, Weaving, Seed, Trellis Couching, Solid Buttonhole, and Bullion

Photograph by Edward T. Howell

PLATE 43   *Curtain.*
Designed by Susan Swan (adapted from Chinese porcelain). Worked by Mrs. William A. Henry

MATERIALS: Wool on linen

COLORS: Shades of green, rose to red crewel yarn

STITCHES: Wheel Buttonhole, Outline, Flat, and Chain

74   *Photograph by Edward T. Howell*

PLATE 44 *Above: Purse, 20th century.*
 Copied from 18-century pocketbook (below), by Susan Swan

MATERIALS: Wool on canvas, silver clasp
COLORS: Peacock green, white, five shades of blue, five shades of brown, five shades of rose, five shades of gold crewel yarn
STITCHES: Florentine (4 up, 2 down). Oval with Cypher, Horizontal Tent Stitch, on canvas. 24 squares to the inch

Below: Man's Pocketbook, 18th century.
 Property of Susan Swan

MATERIALS: Wool on canvas
COLORS: Gold, black, white, peacock blue, green, four shades of rose, four shades of coral, four shades of gold crewel yarn
STITCHES: Florentine (4 up, 2 down). 44 squares to the canvas inch

Photograph by Edward T. Howell

75

PLATE 45 *Valance.*

Designed and worked by Susan Swan

MATERIALS: Wool on linen

COLORS: Six shades of sky blue, four shades of chocolate brown, two
shades of red, five shades of rose, three shades of yellow, two shades
of gold, two shades of mauve, and four shades of green crewel yarn

STITCHES: Outline, Chain, Roumanian Couching, Wheel Buttonhole,
Fishbone, Satin, Trellis Couching, French Knot, Seed, Ladder, Flat,
Long-and-Short Buttonhole, and Solid Buttonhole

Photograph by Edward T. Howell

PLATE 46 *Picture.*

    Designed by Susan Swan. Worked by Mrs. J. Robert Heiks

MATERIALS: Wool on linen

COLORS: Five shades of coral, four shades of honeysuckle brown, and three shades of yellow green crewel yarn

STITCHES: Solid Buttonhole, Spaced Buttonhole, Wheel Buttonhole, Chain, Outline, Satin, French Knot, Fishbone, Arrowhead, Trellis Couching, Roumanian Couching, and Ladder

78   *Photograph by Edward T. Howell*

PLATE 47   *Table Mats, Wild Waterfowl, 12″ x 17″.*
   Designed and worked by Anne Landon Allen

MATERIALS: Wool on beige linen
COLORS: Emerald green, rust, white, blue, purple, grey, green, yellow, and shades of brown crewel yarn
STITCHES: Fishbone, Long-and-Short Buttonhole, Outline, Flat, French Knot, Chain, and Arrowhead

Photograph by Edward T. Howell

PLATE 48   *Background: Bureau Scarf.*
Designed and worked by Mary Taylor Landon
MATERIALS: Wool on linen
COLORS: Three shades each of sky blue, yellow, and grey green crewel yarn
STITCHES: Outline, Flat, Chain, Fishbone, and Fern

Left: Pincushion (clamp). *Designed and worked by Susan Swan*
MATERIALS: Wool on linen
COLORS: Four shades of indigo blue crewel yarn
STITCHES: Solid Buttonhole, Trellis, Fishbone, and Outline

Top: Pincushion. *Designed by Mrs. Emlin Massey. Worked by Mary Taylor Landon*
MATERIALS: Wool on twill-weave linen
COLORS: Four shades of indigo blue crewel yarn
STITCHES: Ladder, Long-and-Short Buttonhole, Wheel Buttonhole, Outline, Trellis, Fishbone, Flat, and Arrowhead

Right: Headband. *Designed and worked by Mrs. John Kurtz*
MATERIALS: Wool on linen
COLORS: White, yellow, two shades of red, and two shades of green crewel yarn
STITCHES: Flat, Seed, Outline, and Fern

Center: Mitt. *Designed and worked by Anne Landon Allen*
MATERIALS: Wool on linen (liner is quilted cotton)
COLORS: Gold, and three shades each of purple and yellow green crewel yarn
STITCHES: Weaving, Outline, Ladder, and Flat

Bottom: Headband. *Designed by Eleuthera D. DuPont. Worked by Mrs. John Kurtz*
MATERIALS: Wool on linen
COLORS: Two shades of brown crewel yarn
STITCHES: Flat, Ladder and Chain   *Photograph by Edward T. Howell*

80

of background stitching to be worked. At present it is almost impossible to buy canvas finer than 24 squares to the inch. Eighteenth-century background materials were generally finer, in the petit-point range of 20 to 45 squares to the inch. The eighteenth-century woman might purchase her canvas with the pattern outline already drawn, but the choice of colors was hers and she worked the entire piece in stitches of her fancy.

An 1803 Boston Encyclopedia defined canvas as "a coarse sort of cloth, of which there are several kinds. Among others are, 1. That worked regularly in little squares, as a basis for tapestry."[28] The article continued, "A cloth of this name, woven less close than those above mentioned, is sometimes used for sieves: hence the verb 'to canvas, to sift, to examine an affair carefully, &c.' "

Both single or mono-canvas and double or Penelope canvases have always been used in America. *The Lady's Manual of Fancy-work,* published in 1859, stated the difference and perhaps a romantic reason for the name:

> It is of two kinds: that in which the threads are at equal distances, which is called "common canvas"; and the sort termed "Penelope," having the threads in pairs, just as it would have were a piece of work in cross-stitch to be picked out often, as we are told was done by the mother of Telemachus. Hence, no doubt, the name by which this canvas is known. For all work in cross-stitch, this will be found easier for the eyes than the other. . . .[29]

Penelope canvas is helpful for the Florentine Stitch and is found as frequently as common canvas in old work.

Stitches commonly used for canvas work of the seventeenth and eighteenth centuries were Tent, Florentine, and variations of the Cross. They are easily differentiated at a glance (pages 104, 117-119). It is more difficult to tell whether the Tent Stitch was worked horizontally or diagonally since the back of old canvas work cannot readily be seen. The Horizontal Tent Stitch is easily executed but stretches the work out of shape on the bias, particularly if the piece is very large. Several old pieces still show this stretching. Canvas work frequently combined a variety of stitches. A piece might contain both Tent and Cross Stitches with French Knots incorporated for accents. As the nineteenth century approached much fine canvas work was done with silk rather than crewel yarns.

Canvas work's greatest asset, its long wearing quality, was fully appreciated in colonial times. A few easy chairs with original canvas work coverings still exist (see Plate 12). It was equally suitable for chair seats, cushions, and men's purses—all of which took a great deal of wear.

Only a few canvas-work rugs of American origin survive. One of these, measuring 18 by 15 feet, is owned by the New York Metropolitan Museum of Art; the daughters of Judge Pliny Moore worked it in Champlain, New

York, between 1808 and 1812. The tablecloth in Plate 13 is an unusually fine, large piece of canvas work. It is not only signed and dated, but its function is clearly named. In England, a few crewel embroideries survive for which matching pieces of canvas work were made. To date, no corresponding American examples have been found.

Old advertisements mentioned "canvas," "canvass," "Canvis," "Canvas Pictures ready drawn," "Cat-Gut," and "scolloping of Catgut."[30] "Scolloping of Catgut" probably meant flamelike or scalloped patterns of Florentine work on canvas-like background. Cross Stitch and Tent Stitch occasionally were mentioned by name.

Special blunt needles and imported background canvas had to be purchased for canvas work and were probably available only in larger cities. The assistance of a teacher seems to have been essential to follow or create patterns. Although it wore well, it was also very time-consuming to work. For all these reasons, canvas work seems to have had a higher status than crewel embroidery.

BERLIN WORK

The popularity of Berlin work in America grew rapidly after its introduction in England about 1805. The needleworker transferred the designs from the squares on the paper to the squares of the canvas. Crewel yarns were used in the early days. A few Merino sheep were brought to America in the last years of the eighteenth century to cross with native sheep to improve the quality of wool in this country. By 1840, the use of Merino sheep had become popular here and their soft wool was used almost exclusively for Berlin work. In 1859, crewel yarn was described in *The Lady's Manual of Fancy-work* as "Fine wool, done up in small, tightly twisted skeins; once very popular, but now but little known, being superseded by the delicate fabrics of the Shetland Islands and the Pyrenees."[31] Yarns made solely from fibers of the Merino sheep were called Berlin or zephyr wools and are easily recognized because of their almost angora-like softness. Any work done here with such yarns must date after 1800.

The canvas was usually 10 to 16 squares per inch, often with special blue threads spaced to aid in transferring squares from the print to the canvas. The most popular stitches for Berlin work were the Tent and Cross Stitch. The later work often combined beadwork with the Tent Stitch.

Pictures by popular artists were the basis for most Berlin work patterns. Homes, castles, and churches were surrounded by sentimental sayings. Both small pictures of flowers and enormous copies of historical and biblical paintings were worked. Slippers, suspenders, pocketbooks, pillows, and footstools were favorite household items worked. After 1840, black backgrounds replaced pale grounds in popularity, which added to the already heavy effect.

About the middle of the nineteenth century, there was a revival of Florentine designs and stitches using the soft Merino yarns. These are frequently monochromatic and seem the most attractive phase of Berlin work.

Many people were derisive of Berlin work even in its heyday, saying it was nothing but copy work of poor designs. Perhaps we find it less appealing because of the unattractive colors. The harmony of colors produced by vegetable dyes was spoiled by the use of mineral dyes after 1820 and aniline dyes after 1856. Harsh magentas, vivid greens, purples, and turquoises were favorites and even faded examples seem strident to our eyes.

MATERIALS

One of the major characteristics of American crewel embroidery is the large expanse of unadorned background fabric (Plate 14). Perhaps because they were often involved in its preparation, American women appreciated gleaming white, plain woven linen more than their English sisters. Moreover, fine linen and wool yarns were costly.

In the early seventeenth century, England permitted her colonies to produce cloth for themselves. Sheep were imported and flax was cultivated. Among the many weavers who settled here was the Puritan Governor William Bradford, who had been a fustian weaver in England. Sometimes individual towns imposed spinning quotas on each family. Fairly simple textiles produced in homes and small factories met the demands of the average colonist.

England, jealous of her own textile industry, became alarmed late in the seventeenth century and imposed restrictions on colonial manufacture. She insisted the colonies produce only raw materials and thus promoted the expansion of domestic English textile manufacture. Among the various laws the powerful woolen industry persuaded Parliament to pass was a curious law requiring that all bodies be buried in woolen shrouds, an edict that remained in force from 1678 until 1814. Passage of the Stamp Act in 1765 and the Townshend Acts in 1767 convinced most colonists that England intended to restrict colonial industries. By boycotting, the colonists made further attempts to increase home and local factory output of cloth. Prizes were awarded and articles published praising families who spun and wove their own cloth. Sometimes they sold their thread for income to local weavers. More often, the housewife took her thread to the town's weaver to be made into cloth for her own use, paying a set amount per yard for the weaving. Few housewives were accomplished weavers, but most communities were served by an itinerant or resident weaver.

Three interesting terms have entered our language from the textile arts: *spinster, towhead,* and *distaff.* The spinster was usually the unmarried

83

woman who stayed with the family and was assigned this tedious job. *Tow* refers to the short, whitish blond pieces that break off and fall when the longer flax fibers are combed. The distaff is a pointed shaft or stick on a spinning wheel that holds the loose flax to be spun; because women were concerned with spinning, gradually the word began to denote the female members of the family.

Linen

Many grades of linen were used for embroidery backgrounds. *Holland* and *kentings,* names unfamiliar today, were types of linens. So were *cambric* and *lawn,* which we associate now with cotton fabrics. A popular twill fabric among the imported materials was *fustian.* Fustian was used extensively in England for crewel embroidery, but few documented American embroideries on fustian have been found. Occasionally the embroiderers used an all-cotton ribbed fabric called *dimity.* Although imported earlier, by 1780 dimity was manufactured in America. Most of the embroidery on this fabric found here seems to have been about this date or later.

From the seventeenth through the nineteenth centuries, families grew their own flax, especially if they were remote from major towns. After harvesting, *retting* (wetting either from the dew for many days or soaking in a stream for a day or two), breaking the outer coating, and hetcheling the long fiber (combing to separate the fibers), it was ready for spinning. Even little girls were taught to spin in both rural and urban communities. In some country areas a father allowed his daughter as much linen thread as she could spin between the publishing of her banns and her marriage. To relieve the boredom of the work, women held spinning contests and spinning parties.

Wool

"Crewels just arrived from London" were frequently advertised for sale in the first half of the eighteenth century. A typical entry is found in the record book of Samuel Powell, a Philadelphia merchant, for "6 pounds of fine cruills in shades" ordered from London in 1724 at the cost of 1 pound 7 shillings.[32]

Wool sheared from the sheep in the spring had to be scoured and carded before it could be spun on the larger diameter type of spinning wheel. The spinner stood and walked to and fro to wind the thread on the spool of the spinning wheel, a more tiring task than spinning linen thread, for which the spinner could sit at her smaller wheel. It has been estimated that a woman could walk more than ten miles a day spinning her expected quota of wool! (Commercial machines that perform this operation are called *mules.*) The crewel yarn a woman made for herself was precious because it had to be as evenly and finely spun as possible for embroidery.

Dyeing the yarn was also a difficult and messy task. Indigo, to make all intensities of blue, was one of the most popular dyestuffs. It is thought that Mrs. Eliza Pinckney brought the first indigo plant to America before the mid-eighteenth century and started its cultivation in South Carolina, where it flourished. Overnight soaking of worsted yarns in indigo produced a medium blue, but a darker blue shade required a week of soaking. Many other dyeing recipes were carefully guarded secrets passed from mother to daughter. They experimented with weeds such as goldenrod, bark from trees, nut hulls, and roots to achieve their shaded crewels.

Because crewel yarns were handspun they always varied slightly in thickness. At least three different weights of crewel yarns can be differentiated in existing work. A few examples wrought with extremely fine yarn and executed with meticulous stitching have survived (Plate 15 and Color Plate II). Today, yarns of this quality are sold as Medici yarns. Most of the eighteenth-century crewelwork used a weight comparable to modern crewel yarns for embroidery and canvas work. A coarser variety of yarn was appropriately used for large motifs embroidered on blankets.

The difficulty of acquiring crewel yarns probably resulted in another major difference in American crewelwork—the frequent use of Roumanian Couching and Flat Stitches in place of the English Long-and-Short or Satin Stitches. In solid design areas, little yarn was wasted on the back of American work even though it meant an extra twist of the needle on every stitch to achieve an effect similar to the more wasteful Satin Stich. (Observe the contrast between the front view, Plate 19, and the back, Plate 20. This pair of curtains is shown in Plates 17 and 18.)

USES OF AMERICAN CREWELWORK

Furniture
Most numerous among surviving examples of American crewel are bed curtains, valances, and spreads. Samples of both coarse and fine work are shown in Plates 16, 21, 22, and 23. Next in importance were cupboard cloths, chair seats, and cushions. Chair seats were of two types, some with solidly worked backgrounds (Plate 24) and others with scattered motifs showing the background linen.

Clothing
Strangely, few dresses ornamented with crewel have been found in the Boston area, whereas at least six survive in Connecticut. Dresses, especially embroidered ones, were repeatedly remodeled as fashions changed and as they passed to other members of a family by inheritance. The child's dress

in Plate 25 may have been cut from a bed curtain. Occasionally, dress material was used to cover chair seats, too. Embroidered clothing was of value enough to earn specific mention in wills. Several dresses are known to have been used as wedding gowns in the days when society did not dictate pure white for a first marriage. Small blankets (Plate 26) were traditionally used at christenings.

Petticoats, an essential part of seventeenth- and eighteenth-century clothing, were decorated with borders of crewelwork. Plate 27 illustrates a portion of a finished example. These borders were sewn at the bottom of a new petticoat until they wore out or the moths had a feast. Many pieces now framed as pictures or panels have probably been cut from these borders in salvaging all attractive motifs from garments originally several yards in length.

The lost pocket made famous by Lucy Locket in the nursery rhyme may have been like the one pictured in Plate 28. Pockets like these held sewing, handkerchiefs, keys, and all the things for which we find a pocketbook indispensable today. Pockets were tied around the waist and worn under the outer skirt, singly or in pairs on the hips. A slit in the outer skirt gave the wearer's hand access to the opening in the pocket. Women also made pocketbooks for men. Crewel embroidered examples are found less frequently than the more durable canvas work (Plates 29, 30 and Color Plate III).

Household Items
Even potholders were embroidered with crewels. Some have survived difficult cooking conditions (Plate 31). Wall pockets, which resembled men's pocketbooks, were hung on the wall by a loop in the top flap. Other items for the house that have survived include hand firescreens (Plate 32), firescreens (Plate 33), pincushions, Bible covers, and pictures (Color Plate III and Plate 34).

Blankets
Blankets deserve special consideration in crewel embroidery. Color Plate IV shows a clever adaptation of the earlier style crewel design using coarser yarns, a larger design, and an attractive color scheme to embellish what would otherwise have been a utilitarian woolen blanket. Several examples exist, found primarily along the Connecticut River Valley, dating from the early nineteenth century. They were both warm and attractive. A fascinating pair, both done by the same woman, survives; one is a bed rug, the other a crewelwork blanket. Both examples are dated, 1794 and 1798 respectively, and are of similar design although worked in different techniques. Perhaps they were intended as summer and winter covers for the same bed.[33] These blankets seem to presage the end of the crewel period and are as charming in their coarse, bold stitchery as the earlier, more delicate work.

86

END OF CREWELWORK

Early in the nineteenth century, advertisements appear offering to teach decorative painting on cloth as a faster means of ornamentation than tedious hand embroidery. The classical revival in furniture forms, clothing, and architecture demanded a lightness and delicacy that complemented shimmering silk embroidery or subtle all-white tambour and stuffed work. Later in the nineteenth century, a heavier, more cumbersome line of clothing and furniture suited the coarser Berlin work done in a mechanical manner from published patterns. The new age of industrialization and mass production placed far less value on handcrafted products. It is said that by the time (1846) the sewing machine was invented to free women of basic sewing, the interest in decorative embroidery had declined.

REVIVALS

An inspiration to Victorian women was the Centennial Exhibition held in Philadelphia during 1876. Displays of old embroidery and furniture awakened people to the beauty of techniques that had long been forgotten. Needlework schools were formed with teachers from England, who taught Kensington Embroidery and Art Needlework, as it was called. This work helped revive the knowledge of fine stitchery, but the designs and stitches imitated the English style of crewelwork rather than the American. Even today English designs and stitches predominate in modern work in this country.

In the 1890's, two women living amidst eighteenth-century houses and furnishings in Deerfield, Massachusetts, admired and began to collect old embroidery discovered in the area. This was an age that re-emphasized the worth of handcrafted techniques. Hoping to help revive some of the town's past skills, they founded the Deerfield Society of Blue and White. Because many of the lovely embroideries had been badly damaged by moths, they decided to do their work with linen thread. At first the Society made only doilies and other small items; later larger items were made on special order. The patterns were never duplicated and each piece was marked with a small flax wheel enclosing the letter *D*. The work of the Deerfield Society led not only to added appreciation for the town's history as a frontier outpost, but was instrumental in reviving a neglected art form. The Blue and White ladies continued to create new pieces until the early 1920's. They were well executed and are highly prized today.

CONCLUSION

Women today have much broader educations, occupational opportunities, and activities than their colonial counterparts. Needlework, however, has continued as one of the most satisfying outlets for feminine self-expression.

The popularity of objects to be embroidered has changed throughout the centuries, but the basic warmth and beauty of crewelwork is as much appreciated today as it was in the past. It adapts easily to period, traditional, or contemporary homes. A room may be decorated around a major piece of crewelwork as a focal point. Equally effective is the use of small pieces as accents in a coordinating role.

We hope that the stitches and designs which follow will provide the reader with ideas and instruction for her own pleasure. Some of the designs are from eighteenth- and early nineteenth-century sources, and others show how these motifs may be adapted for contemporary use. Let your own imagination guide you!

Notes

1. *Literary Magazine and American Register,* III, May, 1805, as quoted in Frank Luther Mott, *A History of American Magazines 1741-1850* (Cambridge, Massachusetts: Harvard University Press, 1957), p. 141.

2. Esther Armes, *Nancy Shippen Her Journal Book* (Philadelphia: J. B. Lippincott Co., 1935), p. 40.

3. *The New York Mercury,* May 6, 1765, as quoted in Rita Susswein Gottesman, *The Arts and Crafts of New York 1726-1776* (New York: The Historical Society, 1938), p. 276.

4. For a more complete explanation of "Dresden work" see L. W. Van der Meulen-Nulle, *Lace* (New York: Universe Books, Inc., 1964), p. 10. See also Margaret B. Schiffer, *Historical Needlework of Pennsylvania* (New York: Charles Scribner's Sons, 1968), pp. 26-35. By 1830 Dresden work was called Moravian work. See *The Lady's Book* (Philadelphia: L. A. Godey & Co., 1830) I, p. 200.

Cat gut, according to *Webster's Third New International Dictionary,* is "heavy linen or cotton fabric that has an open plain weave and is used for stiffening in clothes and for embroidery." See also Ruth Bradbury Davidson's "Needlework" in *Concise Encyclopedia of American Antiques,* Helen Comstock (ed.) (New York: Hawthorne Books, 1958), p. 187.

Crewels were sold "in shades," meaning three or four values of one color.

5. Therle Hughes, *English Domestic Needlwork 1660-1860* (London: Abbey Fine Arts, 1961), pp. 24, 63.

6. *Boston News-Letter,* Aug. 20-27, 1716, as quoted in George Francis Dow, *The Arts and Crafts in New England 1704-1775* (Topsfield, Massachusetts: The Wayside Press, 1927), p. 273.

7. *The New York Mercury,* October 16, 1758, as quoted in Gottesman, *1726-1776,* pp. 276-277.

8. John Irwin, "Indo-European Embroidery," *Embroidery—The Journal of the Embroiderers Guild,* X, No. 1 (Spring, 1959), pp. 8-13.

9. *Collections of the Massachusetts Historical Society,* I, Sixth Series (Boston: published by the Society, 1886), p. 44.

10. Frances Little, *Early American Textiles* (New York: The Century Company, 1931), pp. 220-221.

11. Mrs. Susanna·Condy of Boston said she had "a fine Fustian Suit of Curtains, with a Cornish and Base Mouldings of a beautiful Figure, drawn in London, one Frame full already worked; as also enough of the same for half a dozen chairs." Dow, p. 110. In 1736 Governor Patrick Gordon of Pennsylvania had "fustian wrought curtains for doors and windows." Mrs. Luke Vincent Lockwood, "American Colonial Needlework," *Needle and Bobbin Club*, Vol. 8, Part I, No. 2 (1924), p. 11.

12. Gottesman, *1726-1776*, pp. 293, 275, 277, 278.

13. Dow, pp. 274, 275-276.

14. *Pennsylvania Packet*, September 2, 1970, as quoted in Alfred Coxe Prime, *The Arts and Crafts in Philadelphia, Maryland, and South Carolina 1786-1800* (Philadelphia: The Walpole Society, 1932), p. 45.

15. *Pennsylvania Gazette*, April 4, 1745, as quoted in Alfred Coxe Prime, *The Arts and Crafts in Philadelphia, Maryland, and South Carolina 1721-1785* (Philadelphia: The Walpole Society, 1929), p. 203.

16. *The Lady's Book*, I, p. 156.

17. See Gottesman, *1726-1776*, pp. 277 and 279; Dow, pp. 273 and 276; Ruth Susswein Gottesman, *The Arts and Crafts of New York 1777-1799* (New York: The Historical Society, 1954), p. 293; Moses Judah, cited by Phoebe Phillips Prime Unpublished Index of Philadelphia Craftsmen, courtesy of the Henry Francis du Pont Winterthur Museum; Mr. Buriat, Prime Unpublished Index; and Peter Beraud, Prime Unpublished Index.

18. Gottesman, *1726-1776*, p. 277.

19. Mr. Buriat, *Pennsylvania Packet*, May 3, 1794, as cited by Prime Unpublished Index.

20. Inventory of William Payne of Boston, August 29, 1735. Joseph Downs Manuscript and Microfilm Collection (DMMC), The Henry Francis du Pont Winterthur Museum, Microfilm 12.

21. Little, p. 234.

22. *Boston Gazette*, December 19, 1749, as quoted in Dow, p. 176.

23. *Boston News-Letter*, April 15-22, 1742, as quoted in Dow, p. 273.

24. *The New York Mercury*, September 2, 1765, as quoted in Gottesman, *1726-1776*, pp. 254-255.

25. Alice M. Earle (ed.), *Diary of Anna Green Winslow* (Boston: Houghton Mifflin Co., 1894), p. 12.

26. *Charleston City Gazette*, November 15, 1794, as quoted in Prime, *1786-1800*, p. 260.

27. *Charleston City Gazette*, September 16, 1794, as quoted in Prime, *1786-1800*, p. 220.

28. *The Minor Encyclopedia or Cabinet of General Knowledge* (Boston: printed for West & Greenleaf, 1803), I, p. 231.

29. Mrs. [Matila Marian Chesney] Pullan, *The Lady's Manual of Fancy-Work* (New York: Dick & Fitzgerald, 1859), p. 170.

30. See Gottesman, *1726-1776*, pp. 278, and Dow, pp. 267, 274-276.

31. Pullan, p. 191.

32. Invoice book of Samuel Powell of Philadelphia 1724-25, DMMC, MS M 98.

33. "All Wool and Wide," *Antiques*, November, 1934, pp. 168-169.

II

HOW TO WORK CREWEL EMBROIDERY

*I*n Part II you will find detailed instructions, with diagrams, for working twenty-one crewel embroidery stitches and four canvas-work stitches. Accompanying each stitch description is a design that illustrates how the stitch is used. When you have mastered these stitches you will be able to select and combine them to your taste for working a wide variety of elements and effects. At the end of Part II you will find suggestions for using the stitches, which will guide you further in working your designs.

Stitches and Colors Used Most Often
in Early American Crewel Embroidery

Eighteenth-century American crewel embroidery rarely used more than four or five different stitches in a single piece. Sometimes the needleworker contented herself with only two. Outline and Roumanian Couching Stitches were favored, with Flat Stitch, Ladder, French Knot, Seed, Weaving, Buttonhole, Back Stitch, and Chain Stitches following.

STITCHES

Most Used	Used Occasionally	For Accent or Special Effect
Roumanian Couching	Weaving	Bullion
Flat Stitch	Chain	French Knot
Ladder	Back Stitch	Seed
Outline	Fishbone	Cross
	Fern	Wedge
	Buttonhole (solid)	Arrowhead
	Buttonhole (wheel)	
	Buttonhole (long and short)	
	Buttonhole (spaced)	
	Trellis Couching	
	Satin	

COLORS

Most Used	Occasionally
Shades of blue	Purple
Shades of pink to red	Puce
Peacock blue	Wine
Peacock green	Rust
Shades of yellow	Black
Shades of gold	Coral
Shades of beige to brown	Orange
Shades of green	
White	

The Arrowhead Stitch consists of two Satin Stitches connecting at the apex. It is not necessary to draw lines for these stitches; they may be worked at random.

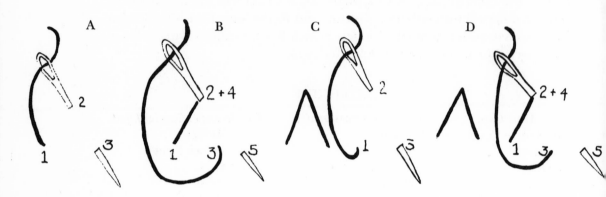

The Arrowhead Stitch may be used for the feathers on the breast and wings of a bird or for filling a large leaf.

Owl, with Arrowhead Stitch

BODY: Outline Stitch, filled with Arrowhead Stitches

RUFF: Roumanian Couching or Flat Stitch

HORNS: Solid rows of Outline Stitch

EYES: French Knot with double thread for center, line around eyes in Back Stitch

A

B

C

D

COLOR PLATE III A *Picture (Adam and Eve).*

MATERIALS: Wool on canvas
COLORS: Beige, three shades of blue, three shades of peacock blue, three shades of coral, two shades of pink, four shades of brown crewel yarn
STITCH: Tent

COLOR PLATE III B *Pincushion.*

MATERIALS: Wool on canvas
COLORS: Yellow, two shades of mauve, three shades of green, three shades of blue, three shades of coral crewel yarn
STITCH: Florentine

COLOR PLATE III C *Man's Pocketbook.*

MATERIALS: Wool on canvas
COLORS: Beige, black, shades of peacock blue, shades of rose-red crewel yarn
STITCH: Florentine

COLOR PLATE III D *Bible Cover.*

MATERIALS: Wool on canvas
COLORS: Yellow, beige, shades of blue, shades of rose crewel yarn
STITCH: Florentine

Photograph by Charles P. Mills & Son
Courtesy The Henry Francis du Pont Winterthur Museum

Also known as Point De Sable Stitch and Stitching.

Work from right to left. Take a short stitch, then insert the needle at the beginning of this stitch and bring the needle out a stitch ahead (A). The stitches do not lap as in the Outline stitch. They meet in the row (B, C).

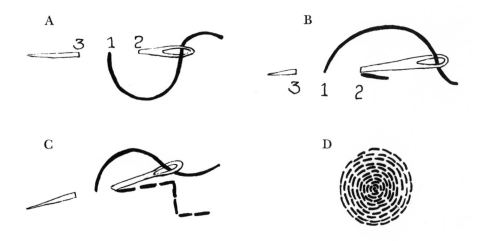

The Back Stitch may be used when a fine line is desired. It is also worked in a coil to form a berry (D).

Flowers, with Back Stitch

FLOWER PETALS: Back Stitch
FLOWER CENTER: Satin Stitch or French Knots
STEMS: Outline Stitch

BULLION STITCH

Also called Wheat Stitch, Caterpillar Stitch, Knot Stitch, Porto Rico Rose Stitch, Post Stitch, Roll Stitch, Worm Stitch, and Coil Stitch.

Take a backward stitch the length required for the finished stitch, but do not pull the needle completely through the material (A). Coil the yarn several times around the pointed end of the needle, usually six or seven times (B). Place the left thumb over the coil and pull the needle gently through the material and the coil (C). Then flip the coil carefully to the right to fill the space of the backward stitch, and insert the needle downward through the material to lock in the stitch (D).

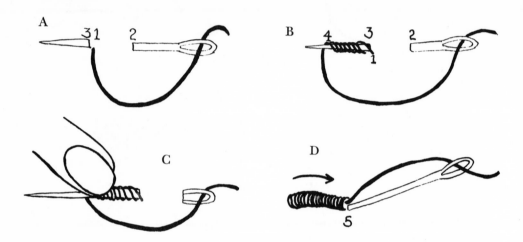

The Bullion Stitch may be used for curls in the hair of a shepherdess or, more often, for the centers of flowers.

Flowers, with Bullion Stitch
FLOWER PETALS: Solid Buttonhole Stitch
FLOWER CENTERS: Bullion Stitch
STEMS: Outline Stitch

98

SOLID BUTTONHOLE STITCH

Work from left to right so that the thread emerges from the lower line. Insert the needle on the upper line and bring it out on the lower line over the thread (A). Hold the thread down with the left thumb while taking the stitch. It forms a straight stitch with a looped edge (B). Repeat stitches may be worked close together as for a buttonhole, or spaced a short distance apart. To end (C) insert needle in bottom line very close to last stitch. Fasten thread on the back of work.

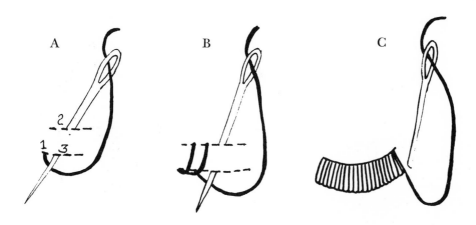

Use the Solid Buttonhole Stitch in working a hollyhock. It is often used when the space to be worked is too small to use the Flat Stitch.

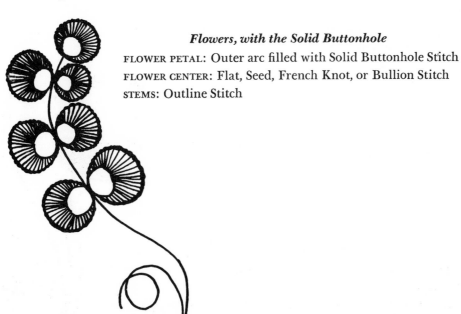

Flowers, with the Solid Buttonhole
FLOWER PETAL: Outer arc filled with Solid Buttonhole Stitch
FLOWER CENTER: Flat, Seed, French Knot, or Bullion Stitch
STEMS: Outline Stitch

The thread emerges from the edge of the circle. The needle goes into the center of the wheel and emerges on the edge above the thread (A). Turn the work with each stitch (B). Do not put the stitches too close together or the wheel will buckle. Use this stitch to fill a small circle (C). The last stitch enters the first stitch to close the circle (D). Secure the thread on the back of the design.

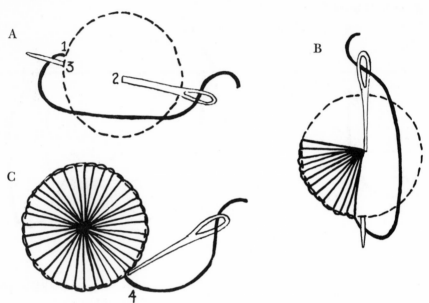

Small berries, grapes, and the faces of bugs are excellent places to use the Wheel Buttonhole.

Flowers, with Wheel Buttonhole

FLOWER STAMENS: Wheel Buttonhole Stitch
FLOWER PETALS: Flat Stitch
STEM: Chain Stitch for heavy stems, Outline Stitch for lighter ones
LEAF: Chain Stitch for vein and Outline Stitch to fill the leaf

LONG-AND-SHORT BUTTONHOLE STITCH

This stitch is worked in the same manner as the Solid Buttonhole (A) except that the stitches are spaced about one-sixteenth of an inch apart with alternating long and short stitches (B, C). To end, insert needle on bottom line and secure on back of work (D).

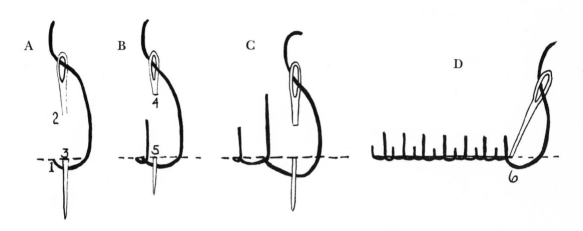

The Long-and-Short Buttonhole Stitch gives the effect of grass when worked on the upper edge of a mound of earth.

Bird, with Long-and-Short Buttonhole

BODY: Solid Flat Stitch
COLLAR: Ladder Stitch
WINGS: Long-and-Short Buttonhole Stitch
EYE: French Knot, with circle in Back Stitch
TAIL: Flat Stitch in upper section, Solid Buttonhole Stitch in lower section

The Spaced Buttonhole Stitch may be worked on the outside line of a leaf or flower. The thread emerges where the stem joins the leaf (A). Insert the needle a short space outside the leaf outline and push it out on the line of the leaf over the thread (A, B). Proceed around the leaf, spacing the stitches about one-eighth of an inch apart (C). To end (D), insert the needle as in drawing and secure thread on back of work.

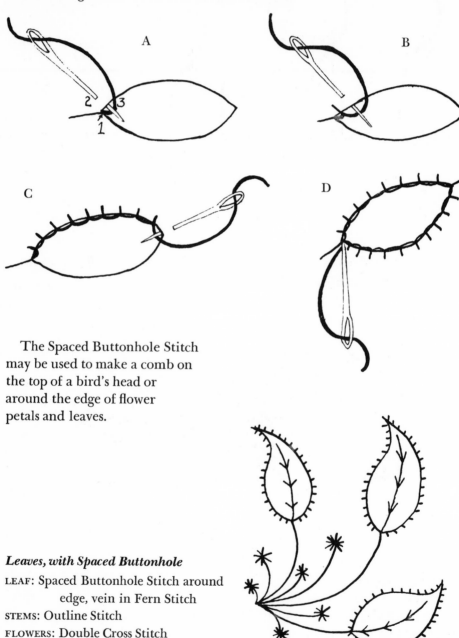

The Spaced Buttonhole Stitch may be used to make a comb on the top of a bird's head or around the edge of flower petals and leaves.

Leaves, with Spaced Buttonhole

LEAF: Spaced Buttonhole Stitch around
          edge, vein in Fern Stitch
STEMS: Outline Stitch
FLOWERS: Double Cross Stitch

Also called Lazy Daisy, Single Chain, and Tear Stitch.

Work from top down. Make a loop of thread by inserting the needle in the same hole from which it emerged (A). Bring the needle out through the loop. Repeat, making sure that each time the needle enters the material it is inside the last chain to lock the link (B, C). To end, the thread enters the material over the bottom of the last loop as close as possible (D). Be sure to work each row of chains in the same direction.

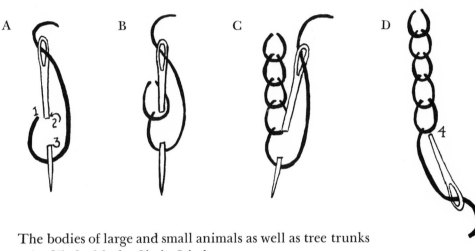

The bodies of large and small animals as well as tree trunks may be filled with the Chain Stitch.

Deer and Tree, With Chain Stitch

DEER BODY: Solid rows of Chain Stitch
DEER TAIL: Fishbone Stitch
DEER EYE: French Knot, using a double thread
DEER ANTLERS: Fishbone Stitch
TREE TRUNK: Solid rows of Chain Stitch
TREE BRANCHES: Flat Stitch or solid rows
   of Outline Stitch

The Cross Stitch is composed of two Satin Stitches. Take a Satin Stitch (A) and cross it with another Satin Stitch of the same length (B, C).

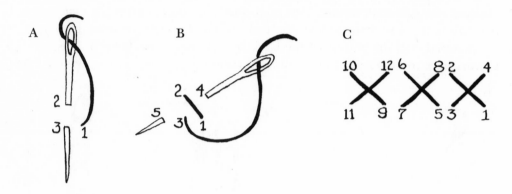

The Cross Stitch may be used as a filling stitch for flowers and leaves.

Flower and Leaf, with Cross Stitch

FLOWER CENTER: Trellis Couching with Cross Stitch to tie down the crossing lines

FLOWER EDGE: Scalloped with Solid Buttonhole Stitch

STEM: Outline Stitch

LEAF (small): Fishbone Stitch

LEAF (large): Flat Stitch on scalloped edge, opposite edge in Outline Stitch, and Cross Stitch to fill the open space

Also called Crow's Foot.

The Fern Stitch consists of a series of three Satin Stitches emerging from the same point. In American crewel embroidery, the Fern Stitch is used instead of the Feather Stitch.

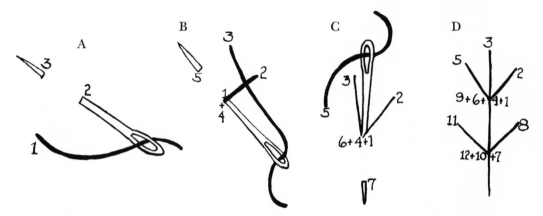

The needle emerges at 1, enters the material at 2, comes out at 3 (A), then returns to material at 1, (which becomes 4), enters matrial at 5 (B), and returns to 1 (which becomes 6). This completes the series of three Satin Stitches. Begin a new series a short distance below, at 7 (C, D).

Peacock, with Fern Stitch

BODY: Flat Stitch

TAIL: Outline Stitch ending with Wheel Buttonhole, and Fern Stitch worked between the rows of Outline Stitch

WINGS: Flat Stitch or Roumanian Couching

LEAF: Outline Stitch, with Fern Stitch for veins

The Fishbone Stitch is ideal for small pointed designs, such as leaves, petals, tails, antlers, etc. Draw a line from the point through the center of the design. Anchor the thread at one end of the line so that the needle comes out at 1 (A). The needle enters the material at 2, emerges on the left at 3, returns to 2 (now 4), and emerges on the right at 5 (B). Fill the design with alternate slanting Satin Stitches (C), working from the center line to the outside of the design. Each new stitch is taken above the previous one until the other end of the line is reached (D).

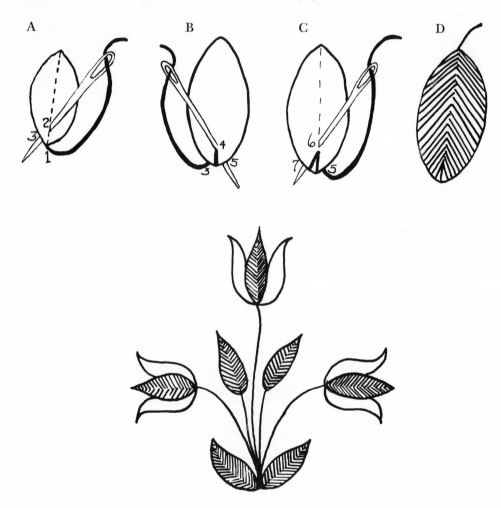

Tulips, with Fishbone Stitch

FLOWER: Fishbone Stitch for center petal, other petals outlined in Back Stitch

LEAVES: Fishbone Stitch

STEMS: Outline Stitch

Sometimes called Economy Stitch.

Work from left to right. The thread emerges on the bottom line at 1, enters the material at 2, and emerges at 3 (A). The needle is then reversed and enters just above the bottom line on 4, coming out on 5 (B). Continue in this manner (C).

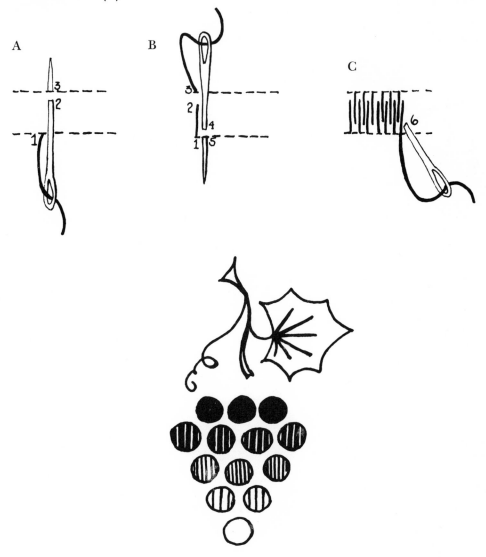

Grapes, with Flat Stitch

GRAPES: Flat Stitch first, then Outline Stitch

STEM: Ladder Stitch

LEAF: Weaving Stitch first, then veins on top in Outline Stitch

FINIAL: Outline Stitch

FRENCH KNOT

Bring the thread through the material at the spot where the knot is desired (A). Hold the needle in the right hand and wrap the thread around the needle once with the left hand (B). Holding the thread firmly with the left hand, insert the needle close to the hole where the thread first emerged (C, D). Secure the thread at the back of the material.

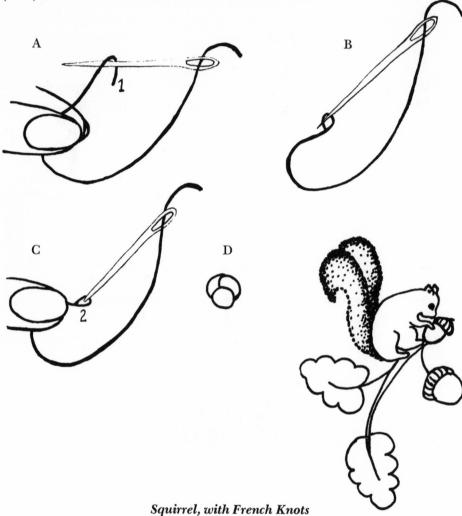

Squirrel, with French Knots

BODY: Solid rows of Outline Stitch, or outlined in Back Stitch with a few Seed Stitches across the back

TAIL: Filled solidly with French Knots worked with a double thread

EYE: French Knots

STEMS: Double lines in Ladder Stitch, single lines in Outline Stitch

ACORNS: Cup in French Knots worked with a double thread, nut in Flat Stitch

LEAVES: Chain Stitch

LADDER STITCH

Sometimes called Herringbone Stitch, Double Back Stitch, Shadow Stitch, Russian Cross Stitch, Long-armed Cross Stitch or Mossoul Cross Stitch.

Anchor the yarn on the right side of the outline and bring the point of the needle out at 1 (A). Then insert the needle a little ahead on the left line at 2, bringing the point of the needle out at the desired distance between stitches, 3. Cross over to the right side and insert the needle at 4, directly opposite the first insertion at 2 on the left side. Bring the point of the needle out at 5, halfway between 4 and the beginning of the first stitch (B). From 5 continue up the ladder from side to side, always bringing the thread out through the hole of the previous stitch. When the distance between stitches is one-eighth to one-quarter inch, the stitches may be couched down where they cross with a small Back Stitch. The Ladder Stitch may be worked in various sizes as shown in C and D.

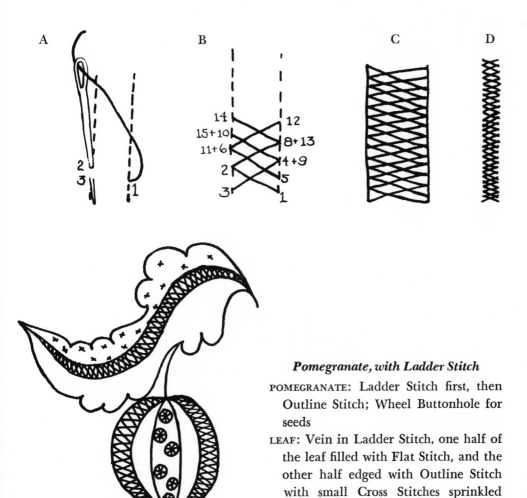

Pomegranate, with Ladder Stitch

POMEGRANATE: Ladder Stitch first, then Outline Stitch; Wheel Buttonhole for seeds

LEAF: Vein in Ladder Stitch, one half of the leaf filled with Flat Stitch, and the other half edged with Outline Stitch with small Cross Stitches sprinkled inside

Sometimes called Stem Stitch, Crewel Stitch, or Stalk Stitch.

The Outline Stitch is one of four stitches used most often in crewel embroidery. Anchor the yarn with several small Running Stitches taken in the opposite direction from the way the outline will be worked. The Outline Stitch is a series of small Satin Stitches worked in a line from left to right. The needle emerges at 1, goes in at 2, comes out again at 1, which is now 3 (A). The needle then goes in at 4 and emerges at 2, now 5, and so on (B). The thread may be thrown either to the right or to the left, depending upon the curve of the design. Always throw the thread with the curve to keep the stitches from falling inward.

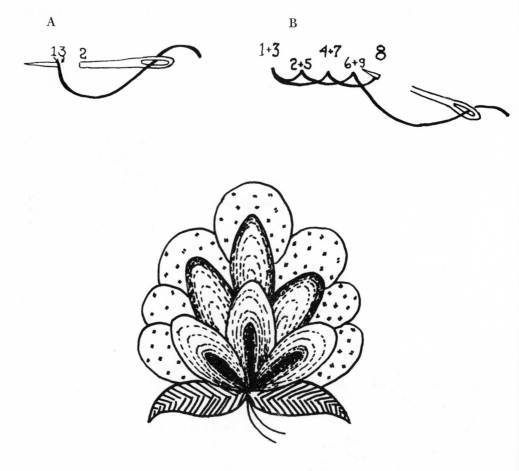

Flower, with Outline Stitch

FLOWER: The six center petals worked solidly in Outline Stitch, the outside petals worked in Outline Stitch on the edge and Seed Stitch inside

LEAVES: Fishbone Stitch

STEM: Ladder Stitch

Sometimes called the New England Laid Stitch, Economy Stitch, Roman Stitch, Oriental Stitch, Antique Stitch, Figure Stitch, Indian Filling Stitch, or Overlaid Stitch.

Working from left to right, the thread emerges on the bottom line at 1; insert the needle on top line at 2, coming out of a short stitch on the left of the thread at 3 (A). Cross over the thread to the right to couch or tie down the first stitch, going into the material (B) a short distance from the bottom line at 4 and emerging on the lower line at 5. Repeat (C). The cross-over or couching stitch should be as long as the space permits, in order to keep most of the thread on the surface of the material. The stitches at both the top and bottom are small. Use the Wedge Stitch with Roumanian Couching as often as necessary, especially on curved surfaces.

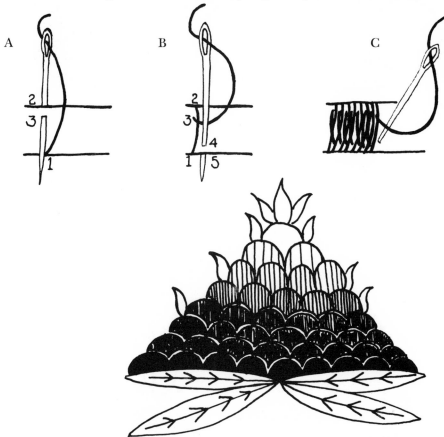

Pineapple, with Roumanian Couching

PINEAPPLE: Segments worked first in Roumanian Couching then Outline Stitch around the outside of each segment

SMALL LEAVES: Fishbone Stitch

LARGE LEAVES: Outline Stitch on the edge, Fern Stitch for the veins

111

The Satin Stitch is used only in a space too small to use Roumanian Couching or the Flat Stitch. The thread emerges at 1, at the lower edge of the space to be filled (A). Insert the needle at 2 and bring it up through the material at 3, very close to the starting point. Repeat with parallel stitches (B) until the space is filled (C).

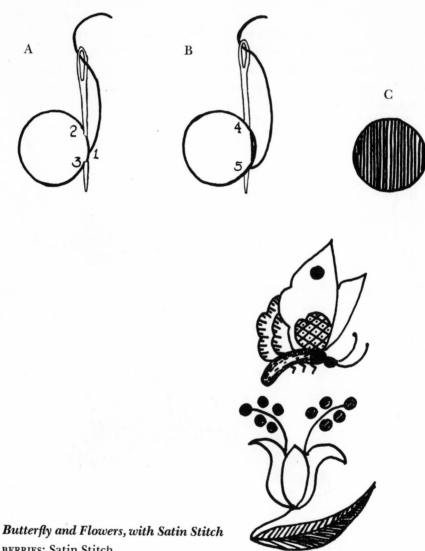

Butterfly and Flowers, with Satin Stitch
BERRIES: Satin Stitch
TULIP: Solid rows of Outline Stitch
LEAF: Fishbone Stitch
BUTTERFLY WINGS: Trellis Couching, Long-And-Short Buttonhole, Satin, and Outline Stitches
BUTTERFLY BODY: Solid rows of Outline Stitch

COLOR PLATE IV *Blanket.*
  American Crewel Embroidery

MATERIALS: Wool on olive-green wool
COLORS: Shades of blue and shades of tan crewel yarn
STITCHES: Outline, Satin, Herringbone, Flat, and Buttonhole

Photograph by Charles P. Mills & Son
Courtesy The Henry Francis du Pont Winterthur Museum

Also called Dot Stitch and Speckling Stitch.

The Seed Stitch is a small single stitch taken in various directions at random to establish an irregular pattern over the area to be filled (A, B). It is important that the Seed Stitches be of the same size to give a dotted or speckled effect (C).

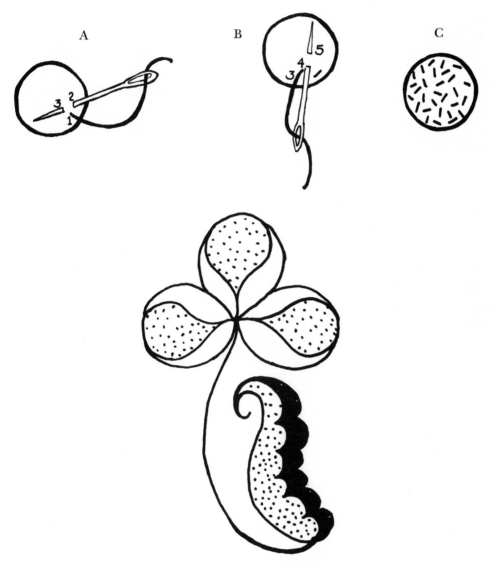

Flower, with Seed Stitches

FLOWER: Solid rows of Outline Stitch, with Seed Stitch in the center

STEM: Outline Stitch

LEAF: Flat Stitch for the scalloped edge, Outline Stitch on the other edge, filled with Seed Stitch

113

Also called Couched Filling Stitch and Squared Filling Stitch.

The threads are laid down in even rows, horizontally and vertically (A, B), and the crossed threads are tied down at all intersecting points. The tying or couching can be a small single stitch or a Cross Stitch, or a combination of both (C, D).

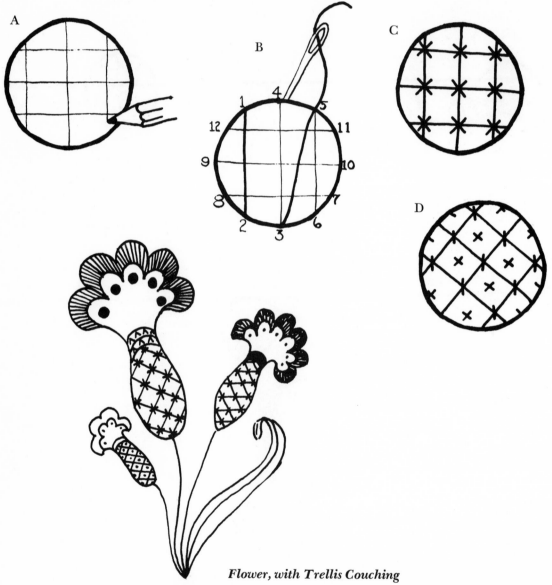

Flower, with Trellis Couching

FLOWER: Outer edge worked in Flat Stitch, large dots in Satin Stitch, small
   dots in French Knot, pod in Trellis Couching

STEMS: Outline Stitch

LEAF: Outline Stitch worked solidly

Sometimes called Running Stitch, Darning Stitch, or Tacking Stitch.

Start the first stitch so that the line of stitches will run through the center of the area to be covered. Pick up one or two threads of the linen with the needle at regularly spaced intervals (A)—the space will be determined by the size of the object. When the edge of the design is reached, turn the material around and run a parallel line of stitches one linen thread away from the first, making sure to pick up the same linen thread or threads as in the center line (B). Repeat until the area is filled (C).

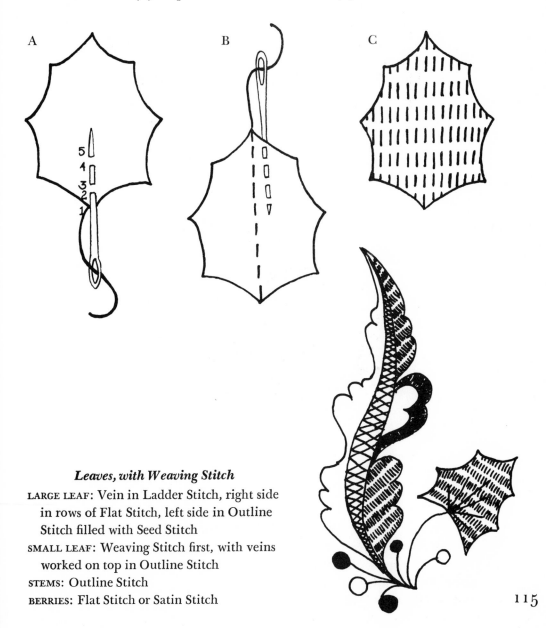

A   B   C

Leaves, with Weaving Stitch

LARGE LEAF: Vein in Ladder Stitch, right side
   in rows of Flat Stitch, left side in Outline
   Stitch filled with Seed Stitch

SMALL LEAF: Weaving Stitch first, with veins
   worked on top in Outline Stitch

STEMS: Outline Stitch

BERRIES: Flat Stitch or Satin Stitch

A short Satin Stitch wedged between Roumanian Couching or Flat Stitches when the outside arc of a design is larger than the inside arc (A). The Wedge Stitch prevents crowding on the inside arc while filling the outside arc, and also keeps the Roumanian Couching or Flat Stitches straight (B).

Flower, with Wedge Stitch

FLOWER: Petals in Roumanian Couching with Wedge Stitch when necessary, center in Trellis Couching, stamens in Outline Stitch and French Knots

STEMS: Ladder Stitch

FINIALS: Outline Stitch

116

FLORENTINE STITCH

Also called Bargello Stitch and Flame Stitch.

The Florentine Stitch is one of the few vertical canvas stitches. The thread emerges at 1, rises four threads to 2, then emerges one thread over and two threads down to the right, 3. The usual formula is four threads up and two threads (diagonally) down. Most of the old work was worked four and two, but occasionally it was three and one, or two and one.

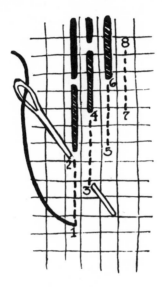

There are two basic designs done with the Florentine Stitch. In one (A), the pattern creates a zigzag horizontal effect. In the other (B), the pattern is a series of diamond shapes. Endless variations of these two themes can be worked out with graph paper. After the first basic outline (the first line in A and rows of diamonds in B) is completed, the color scheme need not be perfectly repeated. In fact, old work rarely had exact repeats of color schemes.

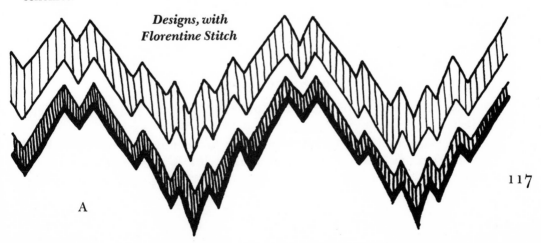

Designs, with Florentine Stitch

A

117

B

CROSS STITCH

Also called Gros Point Stitch.

The Cross Stitch is commonly used for making rugs with coarse canvas. With fine canvas, it is frequently used for lettering and details. Care must be taken to have all the stitches cross the same way. The stitch may cross every thread as shown here, or it may be enlarged to cross two or three threads.

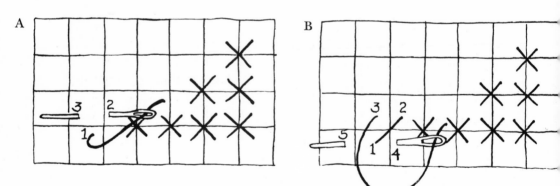

A   B

HORIZONTAL TENT STITCH

Also called Petit Point Stitch, Continental Stitch, and Straight Tent Stitch.

The Horizontal Tent Stitch is good for fine details and pictures, but it will stretch out of shape diagonally if the work is large unless a frame is used. The stitch is worked from right to left. Emerging at 1, the needle goes diagonally back one thread to 2, and moves diagonally forward two threads, emerging at 3. The canvas must be turned around at the end of each row.

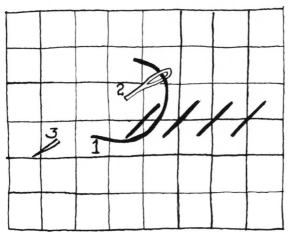

DIAGONAL TENT STITCH

Also called Bias Tent Stitch or Basket Weave Stitch.

The Diagonal Tent Stitch is excellent for large background areas, but it is more difficult to work than Horizontal Tent Stitch for detailed curves. It has two advantages over Horizontal Tent Stitch: the work does not need to be turned at the end of each row, and the work will not stretch out of shape.

The stitch is worked first on an upward diagonal from right to left and then back down from left to right. Going up, the needle emerges at 1, goes back one thread diagonally to 2, and then goes forward two threads horizontally to emerge at 3 (A).

In working back down, assume that the needle entered at (X) on the last stitch towards the top (B). Then it emerges two threads below and one thread to the left, at 1. From there on, the needle enters one thread to the right on a rising diagonal, 2, then emerges two threads vertically beneath, 3.

A

B

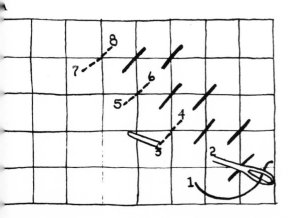

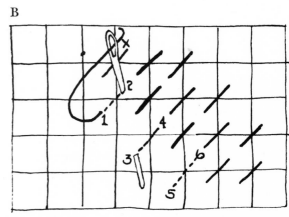

TRANSFERRING THE DESIGN

If the design cannot be transferred with a hot iron, use the following method:

Place the material on a hard-surfaced table. Cover the space for the design with graphite paper. Center the design on top of the graphite paper. Do not pin the design on the material; use four heavy objects such as paperweights to hold the design firmly. Trace the design with a Number 4 pencil. After the design is traced, go over the penciled outline with a ballpoint pen filled with washable ink.

MONOCHROME DESIGNS

A design worked in shades of one color presents few problems. Indigo blue was perhaps the most popular monochrome color used in the eighteenth century. The major elements are worked in the darkest shades and the minor elements in the lighter shades. Try to combine the shades of blue in various ways in the flowers or other objects in the design. The women of the eighteenth century did not seem to have any rules for shading. They combined the shades in a manner that pleased them.

POLYCHROME DESIGNS

When working a design in polychrome, choose several shades of each of the colors to be used. If one color is to be emphasized, use that color to work the object considered to be the focal point of the design. Always work the large objects first. The small objects may be worked in any colors to balance the larger objects.

THREADING THE NEEDLE

Loop the thread over the needle (A). Squeeze the thread very tightly and withdraw it from the needle (B). Still squeezing the thread tightly, pass it through the eye of the needle (C).

ANCHORING THE THREAD

Take several very small running stitches on the line to be worked. Do not leave any tail of the thread showing on the surface of the material. The objection to using a knot in crewel yarn is that it may rub apart and the stitch become loose.

A B

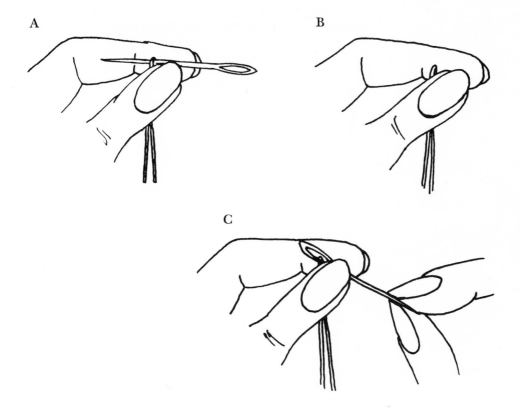

C

ENDING THE WORK

Bring the thread through the material to the back. Secure it on the back with several hidden stitches run in the embroidery. When cutting the thread from the material, leave a three-quarter-inch tail of thread. When the article is washed, if the wool shrinks, it will not pull loose. After it is washed, cut the tails of yarn from the back of the material.

ANIMALS

Bull

BODY: Solid rows of Chain Stitch or Outline Stitch

HORNS: Ladder Stitch (very small) or Outline Stitch

EYES: French Knot worked with a double thread, Back Stitch for the circle around the eyes

HOOFS: Satin Stitch

TAIL: Outline Stitch

Deer

BODY: Flat Stitch or rows of either Chain Stitch or Outline Stitch

ANTLERS: Fishbone Stitch—start at points and work towards center so that stitches will mesh together. Or fill with solid rows of Outline Stitch.

EYES: French Knot, with Outline Stitch for eyebrows
HOOFS: Satin Stitch or Flat Stitch
TAIL: Fishbone Stitch

Dog

BODY: Rows of either Chain Stitch, Flat Stitch, or Outline Stitch. If there are spots on the body of the dog, work the spots first, then fill the body around the spots.
EYES: French Knot or Satin Stitch

Lamb

BODY: French Knot with a double thread. Work a row of French Knots around the entire outline of the lamb. Then, make another line of French Knots just inside the first line. Continue in this manner until the body is filled. This way, the French Knots will be evenly distributed.
HOOFS: Satin Stitch
EYES: Satin Stitch

Rabbit

BODY: Solid rows of Chain Stitch or Outline Stitch
TAIL: French Knot
EARS: Fishbone Stitch
EYES: French Knot

Squirrel

BODY: Outline Stitch or Flat Stitch

TAIL: French Knot

BIRDS

BODY: Flat Stitch, Roumanian Couching, Ladder Stitch

WINGS: Outline Stitch, then fill with Arrowhead Stitches, Flat Stitch, Spaced Buttonhole, or Fishbone Stitch

LEGS: Ladder Stitch (small)

TAIL: Outline Stitch with Fern Stitch worked inside of Outline Stitch. The Ladder Stitch may also be used.

EYE: French Knot

BEAK: Outline

Petals may be worked solidly in the Flat Stitch or Roumanian Couching. To work either of these stitches, the petals must have lines drawn through them approximately one-half inch apart or less. Do not attempt to work the surface stitches in a space larger than one-half inch. The Outline Stitch worked around the finished petals in a different shade is often desirable. If the flower is to be an open design, outline the petals with either the Chain Stitch or Back Stitch and fill with the Seed Stitch.

Carnation

PETALS: Rows of Flat Stitch or Roumanian Couching
POD: Trellis Couching
PETALS: Outline Stitch, then fill with Seed Stitch
POD: Solid rows of the Outline Stitch

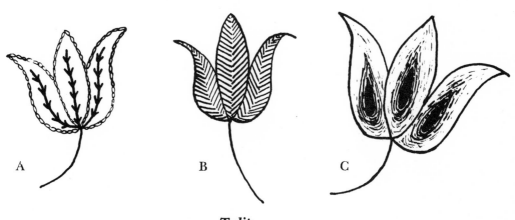

Tulip

PETALS: Chain Stitch around the edge of the petals and Fern Stitch inside
the petal (A), or Fishbone Stitch (B), or solid rows of Outline Stitch (C)

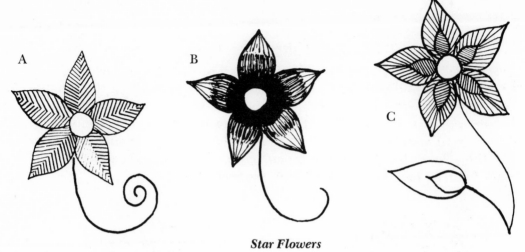

Star Flowers

PETALS: Fishbone Stitch (A), or Flat Stitch (B), or combine Fishbone Stitch and Flat Stitch (C)
CENTERS: Bullion, French Knot, or Wheel Buttonhole

Small Blossoms

PETALS: Lazy Daisy or Single Chain Stitch
CENTERS: French Knot

Strawberry Blossoms

PETALS: Flat Stitch first, then Outline Stitch around each petal

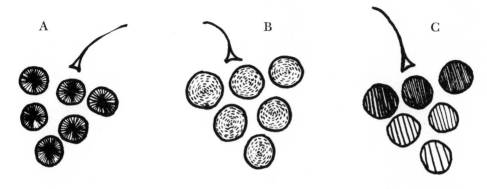

Grapes

Wheel Buttonhole (A), or Back Stitch (B), or Flat Stitch (C). The Flat Stitch may have the Outline Stitch worked around it.

Pineapple

Segments: Flat Stitch or Roumanian Couching, shading from dark at base to light at top, with Outline Stitch around each segment. Leaves: Fishbone Stitch, or solid rows of Outline Stitch (A)

Outline Stitch and French Knots (B)

Segments and Outside: Chain Stitch with a French Knot in the center of each segment. Leaves: Flat Stitch or Roumanian Couching (C)

127

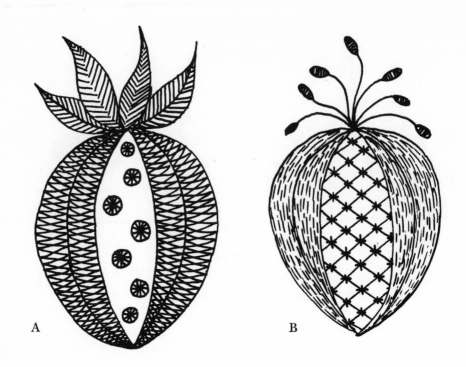

Pomegranate

Outside Segments: Ladder Stitch first, then outlined in the Back Stitch. Center Segment: Seeds in Wheel Buttonhole. Leaves: Fishbone Stitch (A)

Outside Segments: Solid rows of Outline Stitch in different shades of the same color. Center Segment: Trellis Couching. Shoots at Top: Back Stitch, tips filled with Satin Stitch (B)

Strawberries

BERRIES: Fill with rows of Flat Stitch, then add several Seed Stitches worked with a double thread of a different color.

128   LEAVES: Fishbone Stitch

COLOR PLATE V *Chair Seat.*

    Designed by Susan Swan. Worked by Mary Taylor Landon

MATERIALS: Wool on twill-weave linen

COLORS: Black and five shades each of olive green, olive brown, flame red, and marine blue crewel yarn

STITCHES: Cross, Solid Buttonhole, Weaving, Flat, Outline, Roumanian Couching, Fishbone, Chain, Fern and Satin

Photograph by Edward T. Howell

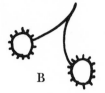

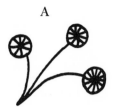

A

B

C

D

Small Berries

Wheel Buttonhole (A), Spaced Buttonhole (B), or Back Stitch (C), Flat Stitch or Satin Stitch (D)

Acorn

CAP: French Knots worked with double thread
NUT: Flat Stitch

LEAVES AND STEMS

Large Leaves

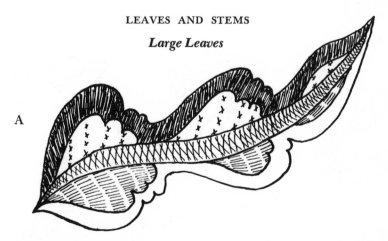

A

Vein: Ladder Stitch. Outer Borders: One side in Flat Stitch or Roumanian Couching, the other side in two rows of Outline Stitch about one-quarter of an inch apart. Inner Sections: Filled with rows of Flat Stitch on one side, and Cross Stitch at random on the other side (A)

129

Vein: Two rows of Outline Stitch with French Knots in the center. Leaf:
Filled with rows of Flat Stitch on one side, the other side edged in Outline
Stitch and filled with Single Chain Stitch at random (B)

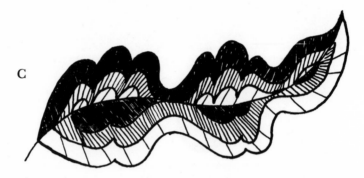

Different shades worked in Roumanian Couching or Flat Stitch—parallel
lines not more than one-half inch apart (C)

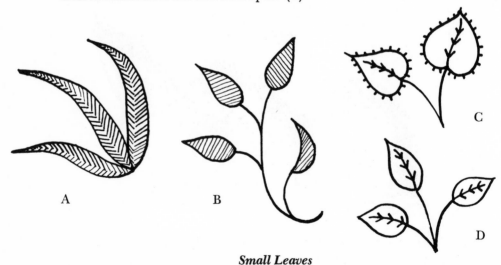

Small Leaves

Fishbone Stitch (A), Flat Stitch (B), Spaced Buttonhole with Fern
Stitch for veins (C), Outline Stitch with Fern Stitch for veins (D)

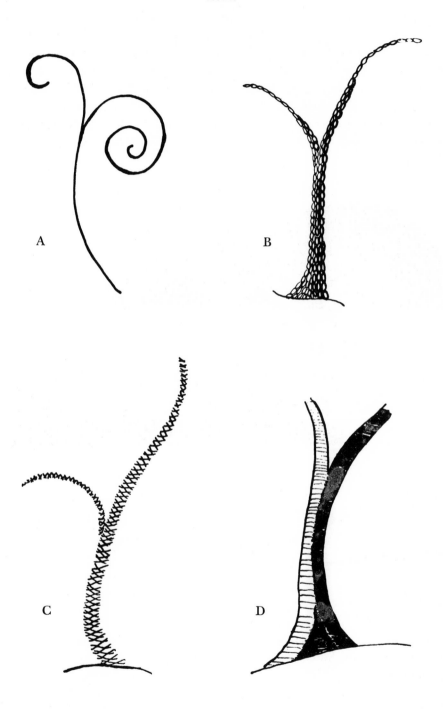

Outline Stitch (A), Chain Stitch (B), Ladder Stitch (C), Flat Stitch (D)

If the design shows flowers or berries in the mounds, work the flowers or berries before working the mounds. When the mounds are to be worked solidly, lines may be drawn around the berries and flowers to fill the mounds with grass. Start at the largest area to be covered, drawing a line one-half inch inside that line. Work from left to right, using either Roumanian Couching or the Flat Stitch to fill that area. Then draw a second line one-half inch from the worked line. Continue to work so that the longer line is below the shorter line, permitting the Wedge Stitch to be used when necessary.

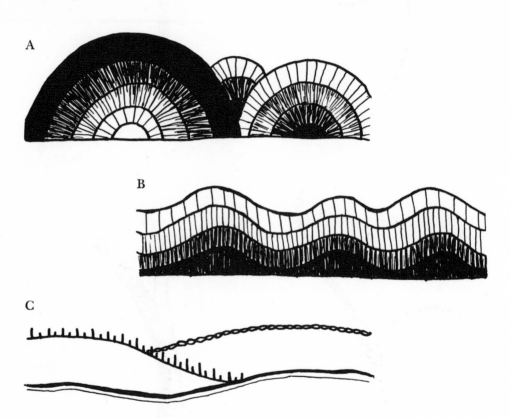

Mounds of Earth

Flat Stitch or Roumanian Couching in shades of one color (A, B), or Outline Stitch, Chain Stitch, or Long-and-Short Buttonhole to suggest rolling ground (C)

III

DESIGNS FOR
CONTEMPORARY
ADAPTATIONS

*T*he photographs and drawings in Part III illustrate the wide range of articles you can create or decorate with your needle—from chairs, pillows, and curtains to purses, pincushions, and pockets. Table mats, pictures, dresses, and sweaters are among the items shown here, and once you have embarked on a project or two, you will begin to see, with a new eye, the scores of heretofore everyday objects that lend themselves to crewel work.

Suggestions for Contemporary Crewel Embroidery

Aprons
Bedspreads
Bell Pulls
Bench Top
Belts
Bureau Scarf
Chair Seat
Clerical Vestments (stole)
Curtains
Dress
Headband
Pictures

Pin Cushion
Pocketbook
Pole Screen
Pot Holder
Sampler
Stool Top
Sweater
Table Mats
Telephone Book Cover
Tissue Holder (pocket size)
Man's Vest
Wing Chair Cover

Chair Seats and Chairs

In designing a chair seat, one's taste is of first importance, although wear and tear should be considered. If the chair is to have constant use, perhaps mounds of earth, or hillocks, across the bottom of the design will give longer wear. Such a design is shown in three stages: above, before being worked; in Plate 35, partially worked; and in Color Plate V, completed.

WORKING A CHAIR SEAT DESIGN

Chair Seat Design

MATERIALS: Wool on twill-weave linen
COLORS: Black, five shades each of olive green, flame red, marine blue, and olive brown

The first step is to study the design to decide which colors and stitches are to be used in the larger objects. At once you realize that the deer is to   137 be worked in shades of gold and tan. Then decide whether you prefer the grapes in the shades of blue or in flame. If blues are chosen for the grapes, the large flower on the right can be worked in the flame color. Keep in mind as you choose the colors that the fourth shade, which is green, will be the predominating color in the mounds and hillocks.

When the deer, grapes, and large flower have been worked, begin to consider the stems. Where the stems are a double line, use the darkest shade of brown in the Ladder Stitch. The single-line stems should be lighter in feeling, and the Outline Stitch in the darkest green will give that effect.

The flowers, berries, and leaves in the hillocks should be worked next in shades of blue, red and gold.

The mounds or hillocks are then filled with rows of the Flat Stitch or Roumanian Couching. Use four shades of green and one shade of gold (olive brown #1). A row of gold is often worked between the greens.

To balance the small berries, acorns and leaves with the larger objects, use shades of the flame color for the sprays of berries, brown and gold for the acorns, and greens for the leaves.

STITCHES AND COLORS

Deer
BODY: Solid rows of the Outline Stitch. Be sure to work the first row completely around the deer. Then move inside that line and work a second row, following the shape of the body. Gold and tan are suggested colors.
EAR: Fishbone Stitch in gold
EYE: French Knot with the Back Stitch around it in black
NOSE: A small Back Stitch of black yarn for the tip of the nose
ANTLERS: Fishbone Stitch in gold. Start a new Fishbone on each tip of the antlers, and work towards the center where the stitches will mesh.
TAIL: Fishbone Stitch in gold
HOOFS: Satin Stitch in black

Grapes
The Flat Stitch is used to work the grapes in shades of blue. Begin at the top and shade the blues from dark to light. After the grapes are filled, work the Outline Stitch around each grape in the darkest shade of flame. The leaves are shades of green worked in the Fishbone Stitch.

Flower
Draw lines one-half inch apart around the flower. Work the Flat Stitch or Roumanian Couching in the five shades of flame. The flower is shaded from light to dark, beginning with the outer edge. Be sure to start the work on the largest arc and work towards the smaller arcs, which allows

you to use the Wedge Stitch when necessary. The leaves on the flower are the darkest shade of blue worked in the Fishbone Stitch.

Strawberries
Fill the strawberries with the Flat Stitch in medium flame. Then add a few stitches of the Seed Stitch worked with a double thread in the lightest green.

Leaves
Large leaf on the left: The Weaving Stitch is worked in medium green, then outlined in a darker shade of green with the Stem or Outline Stitch. The vein is gold worked in the Outline Stitch.

Large middle leaf on the right: A row of the Chain Stitch in the darkest green and a row of the Outline Stitch in light green worked around the edge of the leaf. Fill the rest of the leaf with tiny Cross Stitches in a light green.

Two medium-sized leaves on the right: Fill with shades of green in the Outline Stitch. First work the outside edge of the leaf, then move inside to work the next line. Each line must go completely around the leaf so that the stitch always runs in the same direction.

Acorns
Solid Buttonhole in dark brown fills the cap. The nut is gold worked in the Flat Stitch.

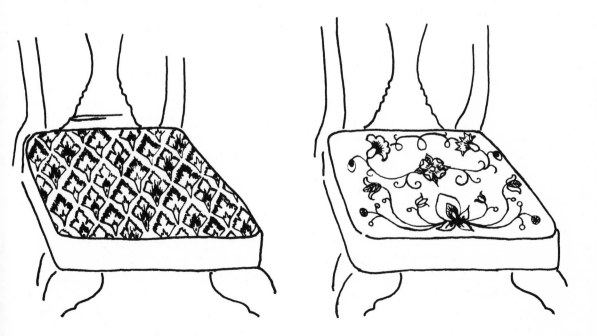

Small Flowers

The tulip petals are worked in two shades of gold. Work a single line of the Outline Stitch and then fill in with the Fern Stitch. The stem is a medium green in the Outline Stitch. The two small leaves are worked in the Fishbone Stitch in a lighter shade of green.

The three small flowers just above the hillocks on the left are worked in medium blue in the Single Chain Stitch. The centers of these flowers are worked in a darker blue in the Satin Stitch.

The remaining flowers in the hillocks are worked in the Flat Stitch. The lighter shades of flame, blue, and gold are used in these small flowers to balance the major objects.

Two other attractive designs are shown in Plates 36 and 37, for comparison.

Dresses or Sweaters

Transfer the design to a piece of net material (such as curtain material) with graphite paper. Do not ink the design to be used for a sweater or dress (A).

Baste the netting onto the right side of the sweater or dress (B).

Work the design.

If a hoop is used, remove it each time the work is discontinued.

When the design is completed, remove the net material by pulling out the threads individually. Do not cut the net close to the design. It is easier to pull a long thread from under the design than a short one. If the thread breaks, use tweezers to remove it (C).

Press sweater or dress on the wrong side.

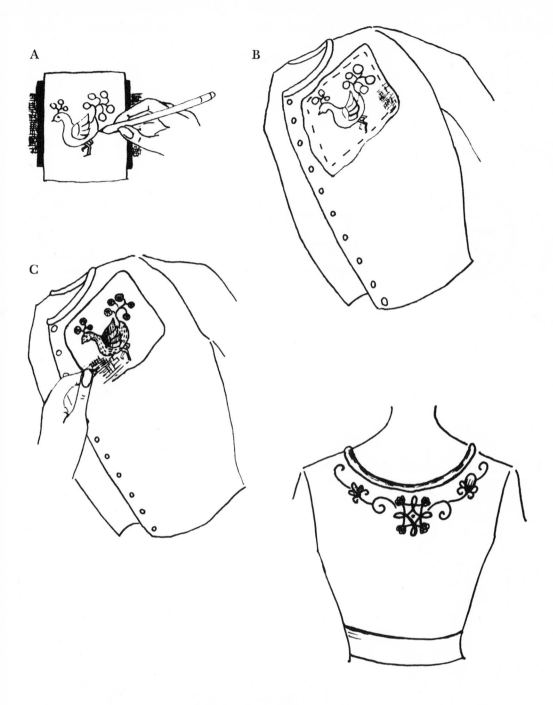

A

B

C

WASHING INSTRUCTIONS

Wash in cool water in Woolite. Do not let material stand in Woolite more than three minutes. Rinse thoroughly, roll in a bathtowel, and let stand no longer than a half hour. Place on a dry bathtowel and iron on the wrong side.

Crewel embroidery may be dry cleaned if preferred.

143

Pocketbook and Purse

144

COLOR PLATE VI   *Child's Sofa, back 23½" high, 32" wide; seat 10½" high.*

Designed by Susan Swan. Worked by Mrs. R.R.M. Carpenter, Jr.

MATERIALS: Wool on twill-weave linen

COLORS: Shades of yellow, blue, green, brown, and pink to red crewel yarn

STITCHES: Bullion, Flat, Roumanian Couching, Satin, and Fern

Photograph by Edward T. Howell

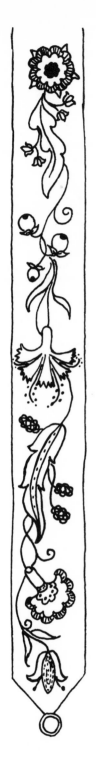

Miscellaneous Small Items

GLASSES CASES

POCKET

WALLPOCKET

POTHOLDER

LUGGAGE RACK

TISSUE HOLDER

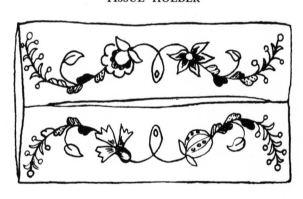

HEADBANDS

147

IV

ELEMENTS FOR MAKING
YOUR OWN DESIGNS

*P*art IV gives you the elements for composing your own designs, whether you wish to work a small headband or an ambitious chair seat. Here are close to 70 separate patterns, almost all of them copies of elements from such eighteenth-century items as a bedspread or a wedding dress. A few are modern adaptations of eighteenth-century designs. You can adapt these elements. along with the more than 100 design elements in Parts II and III in virtually endless combinations.

For your convenience, the drawings are grouped in categories according to the dominant elements—Animals, Insects, and Birds; Flowers; Fruits, Berries, and Nuts; Leaves; and Trees. Many of the drawings include more than one element—for example you will find leaves among the flowers, or trees and flowers in the animal drawings. You can simplify or embellish the designs, or enlarge or reduce them as needed.

153

156

157

158

166

168

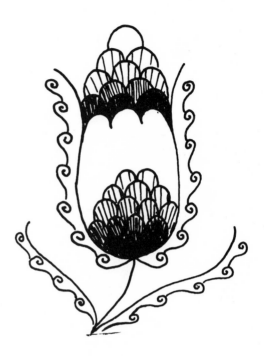

Trees

184

Suppliers of Materials for Crewelwork

Materials for working American crewel embroidery are available in many places. To list all of the suppliers is beyond the scope of this book; however, for the convenience of the reader, it seems appropriate to list a few.

The Metropolitan Museum of Art
(Store)
Fifth Ave. at 82nd Street
New York, N. Y. 10028
  Crewel Embroidery Kits and
  Designs

Museum of Fine Arts (Store)
465 Huntington Avenue
Boston, Mass. 02115
  Transfer Designs

Williamsburg Restoration (Craft
  House)
Williamsburg, Virginia 23185
  Chair Seat and Pillow Kits
  Catalog available

Mrs. Wm. H. Bennethum, III
3601 Capital Trail, Marshallton
Wilmington, Delaware 19808
  Canvas, Paterna Yarns,
  Custom Designs for Needlepoint

The Guild of Strawbery Banke, Inc.
93 State Street
Portsmouth, N. H. 03801
  Linen, Appleton Crewel yarn
  Kits, and Transfer Designs

American Crewel Studio
P. O. Box 553
Westfield, N. J. 07091
  Canvas, Linen, Appleton Crewel
  Yarn, and Designs

The Krick Kit Company
61 Portland Drive
St. Louis, Mo. 63131
  Needlepoint Kits

INDEX

188